Frozen Desserts

Prestige des Grands Chefs

Frozen Desserts

by
Joseph Aimar, Alain Berne and Jacques Joubert

under the direction of
Pierre Michalet
Translated by Anne Sterling

A copublication of

and

Joseph AIMAR

Author Joseph Aimar was born in 1943 in Biot in the Alpes Maritime region. At an early age he decided to be a pastry chef and specialize in candy and ice cream making.

Chef Aimar completed his apprenticeship then worked in several of the top pastry shops in Lyon. In 1976 he won recognition for his work in three important contests. He won the "Medaille d'Or de la Ville de Lyon", the "Medaille d'Or de L'Exposition Nationale du Travail" and earned the prestigious title of "Meilleur Ouvrier de France Glacier."

He then began teaching at the CFA/LEP Francois Rabelais School of Pastry in Dardilly in the Rhone Valley and the "Ecole Nationale Superieure de Patisserie de Yssingeaux" in the Haut-Loire, and at the "Chambre Syndicale des Patissiers et des Boulangers." Chef Aimar also traveled to Osaka, Japan and Jerusalem, Israel to teach his the art of French pastry.

In 1989, Chef Aimar opened his own business, "Les Princes de France" in Champagne-au-Mont-d'Or in the Rhone Valley.

Joseph Aimar is presently a member of the judging panel for the national pastry exams (CAP, Brevet de Maitrise, MOF.) He often participates, with his fellow authors, Alain Berne and Jacques Joubert to demonstrate intricate ice carving.

Alain BERNE

Born in 1954 in Rive-de-Giers in the Loire region, Alain Berne completed his studies in pastry, candy, chocolate and ice cream making in Vienne. He apprenticed at the "Maison Picault", where he was inspired by the chef to dedicate himself to excellence in "patisserie."

After receiving his CAP, he worked with the well known "chocolatier" Chef Bernachon in Lyon and with LeNotre in Paris.

During his military service, Chef Berne turned to cuisine, cooking for the officers and earning his Brevet Elementaire.

Following his service, he worked in the pastry shops of Morin in Meyzieu and Pommerol in St-Chamond. From 1978 to 1987, he joined his fellow authors as an instructor at "Francois Rabelais" in Dardilly. During this period, he earned the prestigious title of "Meilleur Ouvrier de France Glacier."

Presently, Chef Berne teaches at the "Ecole des Arts Culinaires et de Hotellerie" in Ecully, the well known school founded by Paul Bocuse.

In addition to teaching, Alain Berne also participates in the following activities:

- Research on regional French cuisine.
- Founder of a group which researches the history of French restaurants.
- Restaurant reviews (including Alain Ducasse of Monaco, Jacques Chibois of Cannes, Georges Blanc of Vonnas, and Jean Schillinger of Colmar.

Jacques JOUBERT

Jacques Joubert was born in 1948 to a family of wine makers in the Beaujolais region in the heart of Burgundy (in Lyon, Beaujolais is referred to the third "river" of the region, along with the Saône and the Rhône!)

At a young age, he knew he wanted to pursue a career in cuisine and pastry and began his apprenticeship with Jean Lassaigne at the "Croix Rousse" in Lyon. He went on to work in the well known "Au Glacier Parisien" under the tutelage of a Chef Delorme, MOF. It was here that he decided to specialize in pastry. In 1979, Jacques Joubert earned the MOF («Meilleur Ouvrier de France») distinction for himself.

After his military service, he rounded out his skills with work in many reputed businesses: "Beau Rivage Palace" in Lausanne, Switzerland, the Savoy Hotel in London, the "Bayerisherhof" in Munich and "Die Tenne à Kitsbuhel" in Austria.

In 1975, Chef Joubert began teaching at the Rabelais school in Dardilly. This institution has the distinction of working closely with students from the beginning of their apprenticeship to the final training for a permanent position.

In 1989, Chef Joubert managed the famous "Pâtisserie de l'Horloge" in Tassin la Demi-lune in the Rhône region and directed operations at the "Confiserie du Vieux Lyon" which produces several chocolate specialties of the region, notably the "Pavés de Vieux Lyon», "Écussons de Lyon" and the "Gros Caillou de la Croix-Rousse."

Joseph AIMAR

Alain BERNE

Jacques JOUBERT

Note from the editor

«Frozen Desserts» is a collaborative effort of an exceptional team of talented French «glaciers».

Beyond the professional accomplishments of each, the chefs are the ideal authors for this book for the following reasons:

All three authors worked together as instructors of pastry and ice cream making at the distinguished school, «Lycee Rabelais» of Dardilly.

The authors are very well rounded chefs. In addition to their specialized talents in «glacerie», they each have been trained in pastry, chocolate, candy making and cuisne.

Together they formulated new ideas to inspire their students and each of the authors has shown a special interest in the young chefs of tomorrow and encourage their students to seek training in all fields of cooking.

Foreword from President Jean CABUT

What a wonderful idea to produce a book featuring frozen desserts. This will be an invaluable resource for professionals as well as amateur cooks.
The highly qualified authors, all «Meilleurs Ouviers de France », have shared their many years of experience to bring to the readers classic as well as innovative ideas for serving ice creams and sorbets.
Of special interest to professional restaurant chefs and pastry shop owners, the ideas in this book will inspire your own creations and expand your repertoire.
Original desserts such as these will attract attention from your customers and make a name for your enterprise.
My compliments to Joseph Aimar, Alian Berne and Jacques Joubert and congratulations to the publisher, Éditions St Honoré. This book brings the highly skilled work of experienced chefs to a wide audience and a renewed respect for our industry.
I wish you all great success.

Foreword from President Daniel MENAND

This book will acquaint you with sorbets, ice cream and specialty frozen dessert.

As president of the «National Confederation of Ice cream Makers of France», I salute your work with these noble ingredients.

Our profession is indebted to you for showing the variety of possibilities in this branch of the culinary profession.

Thank you to the authors for creating such creative dishes with the ice creams, sorbets and other frozen confections that our confederation takes such pride in. You all do honor to your prestigious titles of « Meilleurs Ouvriers de France » Glacier.

Jean CABUT
Président
Confédération Nationale de la Boulangerie et Boulangerie-Pâtisserie Française

Daniel MENAND
Président National
Confédération Nationale des Glaciers de France

Table of Contents

Arlette Goubier

Chapter 1 - Preparation of Ice Creams and Sorbets

In the realm of «Haute Gastronomie», frozen desserts are considered among the most refined preparations. There has always a great deal of interest in this field and innovations are continually made to diversify and improve frozen desserts.
The volume of frozen desserts served in tea rooms and restaurants has increased by 20 times over the last two decades.

History of ice cream

Man started chilling foods and making frozen confections thousands of years ago.
The Egyptians discovered that foods placed in earthenware pots could be cooled by evaporation with large fans.

In northern regions, man learned how to "harvest" ice from the frozen lakes and store it throughout the warm months. They broke the surface of the ice and carried the blocks of ice to deep holes in the ground lined with straw. More straw was placed between the layers and on top to provide insulation. Several tons of ice, stored in this fashion could stay frozen for many months.

This ice was usually reserved for making desserts for the wealthy families. The servants pounded the ice to a snowy consistency and combined it with honey and fruit juices to make a rudimentary sorbet.

As time went on, the ice was used to freeze mixtures of eggs, milk and honey. To drop the temperature of the ice, salt was added and the bowl of custard was placed on top. As the ice melted the ice cream mixture was stirred by hand.

Honey remained the major sweetener for many years. Sugar was very scarce and sold as a medicine until Napoleon 1st came into power. Among the many advances in food production during this period were new techniques in making beet sugar developed by Benjamin Delessert.

With each discovery of a new technique or ingredient, ice creams and sorbets became more refined and could be enjoyed by more people. From distant lands came vanilla, chocolate and exotic fruits, adding a new dimension to desserts of all kinds. Electricity changed the face of cooking forever. "Glaciers" could now use a powered churn instead of hand cranking their ice cream. Refrigeration slowly improved, first using liquid ammonia which was replaced with freon which is dependable and safe.

With the development of more and better machinery, ice cream making became a year round industry, with products affordable to all people. Progress brought better hygiene. Louis Pasteur's research in bacterial growth began a whole new era of food products to the masses.

Advances continue to be made which improve the quality and availability of frozen desserts such as the invention of the ice cream cone which spawned the huge industry of portable ice cream.

"Glacerie": Ice cream making becomes a modern industry

With advanced technology and reliable ingredients, ice cream making has become a science, with dedicated professionals continuing to make improvements that benefit producer and consumer.
Government legislation has contributed greatly to the quality of frozen confections by setting standards for ingredients and production. Stabilizers made of gelatin and alginates have improved the texture, taste, volume and self life of frozen products.
New sweeteners such as powdered glucose improve the flavor and inverted sugar such as trimoline improve the texture of fruit sorbets and ice cream mixtures made with egg yolks.

Ice cream and sorbet, a healthy dessert

Ice creams and sorbets made with high quality ingredients provide a wide range of nutrients. In addition to being a treat fit for a king, well made ice cream and sorbets has many virtues.

● Ice cream has a calming effect on the nerves and relaxes muscles to create a feeling of well being.
● Ice cream is nutritious: contains vitamins, minerals, protein and a high percentage of water. Ice cream is an excellent high calcium treat for children.
● Sorbets are often made with fruit high in Vitamin C, an important vitamin for combating infections.

After so many years of being a fancy dessert reserved for the privileged few, frozen desserts have become a treat we can all enjoy in good health.

A profitable business

Ice creams and sorbets are products made with relatively inexpensive ingredients that can be stored efficiently. The turnover in a well run shop is quick and the profits can be quite high. Fresh fruits purchased in season, are not only at the height of flavor but at their lowest price.

The basic ingredients of ice cream, milk, sugar and eggs are reasonably priced and available year round.

These simple ingredients become profitable when the skilled chef transforms them into smooth, creamy confections and presents them beautifully.

Automated equipment aids the chef in facilitating the production of large quantities of high quality ice cream and sorbets..

The personality of the chef really shines in the final stage when various mixtures are combined to create original desserts.

This volume, "Frozen Desserts" is designed to inspire cooks to try new ideas and perhaps create frozen desserts of their own.

Ingredients used to make ice creams and sorbets

One of the fascinating aspects of ice cream making is that such wonderful dishes are made with such simple ingredients.
In chapter 6, the basic ingredients are grouped by category to supplement the information given here.
The steps required for making frozen desserts are not complicated either, however each step is important:
- Choosing the freshest ingredients
- Careful preparation
- Skilled assembly

1. Fruits

a/ Fresh fruits
Fresh Fruits are used in many forms: poached, puréed, macerated, or in juice form. They can be processed «in house» or high quality products can be purchased in cans or frozen. Fruits are sometimes the main ingredient or serve to add flavor and color. As a garnish, they can be chopped and macerated so that the texture remains soft when frozen.

Always choose ripe, unblemished fruit and wash well in cold water before using.

b/ Candied fruits
Fruits cooked in sugar will not become hard and icy when frozen, making them a very good choice for decorating frozen desserts of all kinds. Chopped candied fruits can also be stirred into ice creams and parfaits to add flavor and texture to the mixture.

c/ Nuts
Nuts can be added as a chopped garnish to a frozen mixture or ground to a paste and added as a main flavoring ingredient. The fat content of nuts is very high so they should be used in small quantities.

2. Milk products

a/ Milk
Milk, the principle ingredient in ice cream is used in many forms in French «glacerie»: pasteurized, long conservation, powdered, and concentrated.
The milk called for in the recipes of this book is pasteurized whole milk.
If other types of milk are used, the recipes should be adapted accordingly.

b/ Cream
Heavy cream or whipping cream most closely resembles the «creme liquid» used in France to make ice creams. Creme fraiche is too acidic to be used in these preparations.
Cream or butter is almost always added to ice cream mixtures to raise the fat content which makes the ice cream smoother and richer. For certain products to be labeled «crème glacée» or «glace aux oeufs» in France, they must contain a minimum amount of butterfat.

c/ Butter
Butter (unsalted) is sometimes used with or instead of cream, to add richness to ice cream mixtures. It is especially good in coffee ice cream.

3. Eggs

The eggs called for in these recipes are large, grade A. Only the yolks are used, which emulsify with the milk to add smoothness. In small amounts, egg yolks add a desirable color, flavor

and texture, but too many eggs can overpower the taste and make the frozen product too hard and dry.

4. Sugar

a/ Sugar (saccharose)

Basic sweetener for most ice creams and sorbets. The amount is closely regulated by the French government.

The ratio of sugar should be regulated according to the other ingredients (very ripe fruits, for example) to achieve the perfect balance of flavor and texture:

- Too much sugar = flavor too strong; frozen product may not freeze properly and may be too dry.
- Not enough sugar = bland flavor and icy texture.

b/ Trimoline (inverted sugar)

Trimoline is made from saccharose which has been divided into glucose and fructose. Trimoline is 20% sweeter than saccharose. It is therefore used in small quantities. This ingredient improves the texture of ice creams and sorbets, making them smoother. The acidity in trimoline adds flavor and helps to maintain the color.

5. Flavorings and Colorings

a/ Flavorings

Ice cream can be flavored with chocolate, vanilla, praline, caramel and coffee just to name a few. Choose fresh, high quality flavorings for the best results. The amount used depends, in part, on the level of quality of the finished product.

b/ Aromatics

A wide assortment of herbs and spices can be infused into ice cream and sorbet mixtures to augment the flavor: mint, cinnamon, jasmine, lavender and tea, for example. One delicious dessert in this book calls for finely chopped mint with sugar between layers of parfait.

c/ Extracts

Extracts, used widely in baking in the US. are used only occasionally in French «glacerie», added to cooled custards to add a little extra flavor.

d/ Coloring

Natural food color is used only to correct or enhance the color of ice creams when necessary.

Products made with fresh, high quality ingredients rarely need to be improved with food color.

6. Wines and liqueurs

A wide variety of wines and liqueurs can be used to flavor ice creams and sorbets.

The dose must be just right or the taste and texture won't be good. Too much alcohol ruins the taste and also raises the freezing temperature. Robust red wines especially do not blend well with sugar and don't freeze well, red wine sorbet is best made with a light, medium quality wine.

7. Stabilizers

Various stabilizers have been developed for the ice cream industry which minimize the formation of ice crystals, making the frozen mixture smoother. As the mixture sits and develops flavor, the stabilizer will swell slightly, increasing the volume. Stabilizers also give body to the ice cream which holds it together as it softens.

Optional in artisan preparations, it is necessary only when the product will be stored for a long period.

Stabilizers authorized in France include: agar agar, pectin, gelatin, egg white, carob and alginates.

Diglycerides are sometimes used as an emulsifier.

Tools and equipment used to make frozen desserts

This list of tools and equipment includes those particular to French «glacerie». The general tools used by cooking and pastry chefs such as spatulas, bowls, ovens and refrigerated counters are not included.
In the last section of this book there is a more detailed description of some of the professional machines used in French ice cream making such as the churn and pasteurizer. Each enterprise needs to purchase equipment that is suitable to the quantities and style of preparation.

1. Small tools and equipment
a/ Molds

The assortment of molds available to the "glacier" is expanding all the time. Any recipient made of metal or plastic that conforms to government standards can be used.
See different types of worlds in Chapt. 6

b/ Specialized equipment
● *Ice cream scoop:* Scoops are available in graduated sizes to portion scoops for ice cream cones and desserts such as "Pineapple Harlequin.» Each size scoop yields a varying number of portions per liter, so that stock can be controlled.
● *Conical strainer* (fine-meshed or metal), also known as a "China cap": Used to strain sauces such as crème anglaise (custard), fruit purées and juices, syrups, etc.
● *Whipped cream dispenser:* Used primarily in tea salons in France where fancy ice cream sundaes are served, the whipped cream or "crème Chantilly" can be applied quickly and in pretty designs.
● *Mixer:* Indispensable piece of equipment which allows the "glacier" to blend and whip mixtures quickly and with the same results each time. Used for meringues, bombe mixture, sponge cakes, mousses and more.
● *Food processor:* Used for chopping solid ingredients as finely or coarsely as needed and making nut pastes.

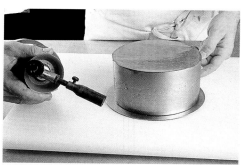

● *Juicer:* Used for making fresh fruit juices and purées.

c/ Measuring tools
● *Scale:* Indispensable tool in the French kitchen (especially pastry, candy and ice cream making) where every ingredient is weighed. Choose a well made and solid scale and check for precision periodically.

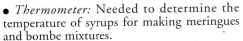
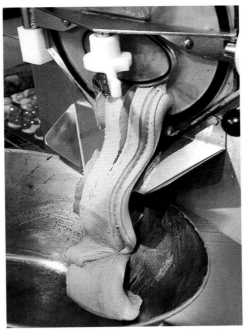

● *Thermometer:* Needed to determine the temperature of syrups for making meringues and bombe mixtures.

● *"Densimetre"* (hygrometer): Used to determine the amount of water in a sugar syrup. . The average density used in sorbets is 1147 D.

● *"Refractometre»*: Serves the same purpose as the "densimeter», measures the sugar solution to achieve smooth, delicious results.

● The choice of dishes for serving the frozen desserts is very important. The plates, bowls and "coupes" (glasses) must withstand freezing temperatures and the heat of the dishwasher. In France, a wide variety of attractive yet robust lines of dishes are available for the professional "glacier.»

2. Large equipment

a/ Churn

The churning device is one of the most essential pieces of equipment in the "glacier's" kitchen.

The professional, large-scale model consists of a cylindrical bowl which turns in a cooling unit. A paddle with two arms is turned from the top in the opposite direction. As the liquid in the bowl freezes around the sides, the paddle scrapes it off and stirs the frozen solids into the mass. In France, these expensive machines come in a variety of sizes so that a business can match the capacity with its production level.

Small restaurants that want to offer one flavor of homemade ice cream on their dessert menu can purchase a one liter machine which makes just enough each day and does not take up too much room.

"Sorbetière" (small churn for home use)
For the home cook who enjoys freshly churned ice cream, the old-fashioned churn which required ice layered with salt to successfully chill the cylinder, has been replaced by a new device with a coolant which lines the metal bowl that can be frozen in advance.

The results are never quite as good as the professional machines which keep a constant

temperature and churn the mixture at an even speed. The smaller devices, whether powered by a small motor or by a hand crank cannot match the dependability of the larger, self contained churns.

However for occasional ice cream making, these smaller machines are a much less expensive alternative. With their popularity on the rise, however, many inferior models have been placed on the market, so buyer beware.

b/ Pasteurizer

French legislation demands that all ice cream produced for sale to the public be pasteurized to eliminate all possibility of bacterial contamination. This process can be achieved through proper cooking techniques and also with a devise made specifically for that purpose. This sophisticated machine processes 5-6 liters (about 6 quarts) at a time, first heating the mixture to the proper temperature for a predetermined amount of time, then chilling the mixture very quickly thus eliminating the

lengthy process of stirring the mixture over ice to cool it. Some machines combine the pasteurizing and cooling process with churning so that the freshly cooked custard can be placed in the machine to be pasteurized, it is cooled then perfectly churned with no need for the cook to intervene.

c/ Freezer

Specialized sub zero freezing units are used in professional ice cream making which bring down the temperature of the frozen desserts as quickly as possible. This enables the chef to make some desserts in advance and hold them with no deterioration in quality. For this reason, this piece of equipment is sometimes referred to as the "conservateur" or "conserving device.»

The chilling is done in two stages, first lowering the temperature to -35 C (-31 F) then storing them at -25 C (-6 F.)

For fresh ice cream at home, the freezer compartment of the refrigerator conserves perfectly well for short periods of time.

Preparing scoops of ice cream

Ice cream scoops come in a variety of styles, sizes and qualities. The method for using them to make a perfect scoop is the same.

1. Fill a bowl with warm water and dip the scoop into the water before forming each scoop. This washes the scoop off and warms it a bit to make it easier to insert the scoop in the ice cream.

2. To form a perfect round shape, scrape the surface of the ice cream with the edge of the scoop. The layer of ice cream follows the contour of the scoop to make a ball.

3. Position the scoop over the cone or in the center of the service plate and release the ice cream with a squeeze of the handle.

4. Rinse the scoop in warm water before making another scoop.

At an ice cream stand, it is a good idea to have several scoops in containers of warm water.

Molding small shapes

Another popular way to present ice creams and sorbets in France is in the shape of fruits, animals, flowers and other forms.

The molds, which come in a variety of sizes were traditionally made in bronze with an aluminum lining. In recent years, plastic molds which meet sanitary standards have become available.

The metal molds can be placed in the freezer in advance so that if the ice cream is a little soft (which makes molding into the intricate design a little easier), it will firm up immediately. Also the metal molds can be warmed slightly for unmolding. The plastic molds can be pulled away from the ice cream to release it.

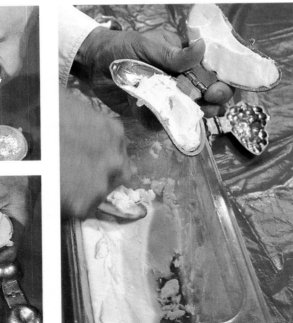

Cookies, the perfect accompaniment to ice cream

A cookie of some kind is always served with ice cream desserts in France. Although any crisp cookie can be served with frozen desserts there are a few types that have become traditional.

One of the most popular types is the simple batter of egg whites, sugar, butter and flour which can be molded around a spoon handle to make "cigarettes», over the bottom of a small soufflé dish to make a "tulip" (which serves as an edible bowl) or simply piped in strips to make "langue de chat" («cat's tongue».) The recipe is included in the last section.

Puff pastry "palmiers" («elephant ears»), butter cookies from Brittany and flaky fan-shaped cookies are also popular.

Arlette Goubier

Chapter 2 - Frozen Desserts made with Scoops of Ice creams and Sorbets

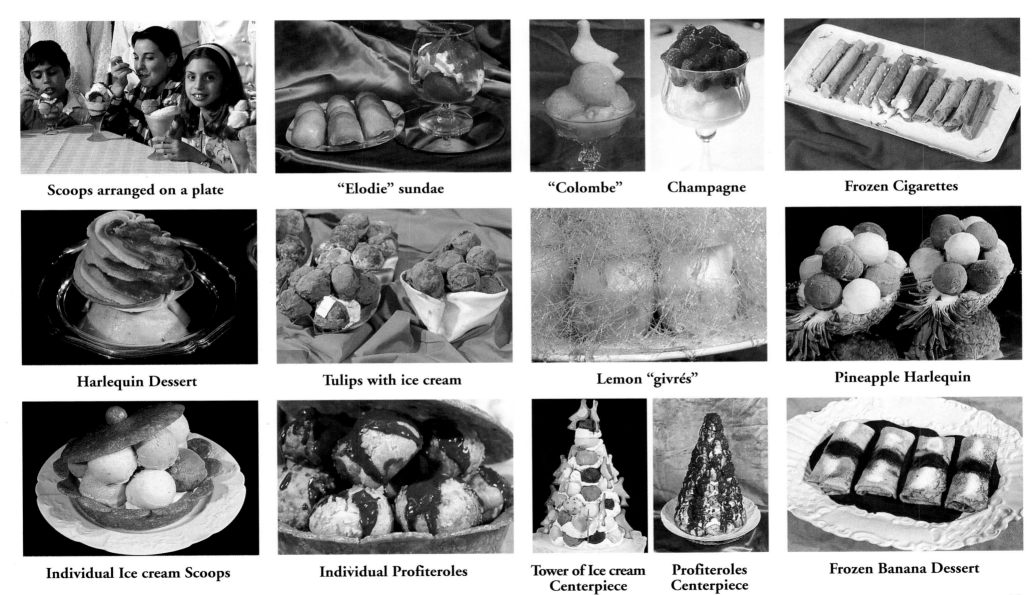

Scoops arranged on a plate

"Elodie" sundae

"Colombe"

Champagne

Frozen Cigarettes

Harlequin Dessert

Tulips with ice cream

Lemon "givrés"

Pineapple Harlequin

Individual Ice cream Scoops

Individual Profiteroles

Tower of Ice cream
Centerpiece

Profiteroles
Centerpiece

Frozen Banana Dessert

Ice cream cones

Ice cream cones are not just a summertime dessert for children. Anytime, anyplace, everyone enjoys this portable treat. First served at the World's Fair in Paris in 1900, serving a scoop of ice cream in an edible cone has become popular throughout the world. The tradition in France is to serve small scoops of intensely flavored ice creams and sorbets. The most notable «glaciers» in the country offer a staggering variety of interesting flavors.

Choosing the right cone

In France there are many types of cones to choose from.
● The "glacier" first matches the size of the cone to the size of the scoop he plans to serve and chooses among the many designs.
● Since the cone is like a cookie served with the ice cream, it should be delicious to eat as well.
● The cone needs to be sturdy enough to not disintegrate while the ice cream is being eaten.

Choosing flavors that go well together

Mixing two or three flavors of ice cream and sorbets on one cone is part of the fun, especially for children.
While almost any combination can be delicious if the ice cream is well made, there are classic marriages that work especially well.
In Chapter 6 some of the best combinations are listed.

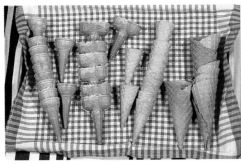

Ice cream sundaes

Scoops of ice creams and sorbets served in a dish can be a simple dessert consisting of a few flavors and a dollop of whipped cream. The scoops can also be embellished with any number of sauces and garnishes to create sundaes which express the personality of the chef. Whether you've made the ice cream yourself or purchased a variety of flavors to assemble at home, creating sundaes is a pleasure for everyone.

Three criteria determine how the sundae will come out:
- The flavors on hand.
- The form and size of the scoops.
- The sauces, garnishes and decorations on hand.

With these elements to work with, each sundae can be an original creation, mixing and matching flavors, colors, and shapes to suit the occasion and tastes of the guests.

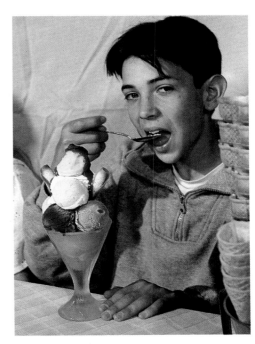

Serving ice cream and sorbets on a plate

A large plate can serve as the canvas for a culinary work of art.
The «artist» should first choose a plate that will harmonize with the colors of ice cream and sorbets.

If a fancy garnish is planned, the plate itself should not have an elaborate design. The rim of the plate should «frame» the arrangement of ice cream and decorations without taking away from the colors and forms of the food.

Colorful sauces can be placed on the plate underneath the scoops of ice cream or piped with a paper cone in pretty designs.

Fruits, cut in attractive shapes and fancy cookies can be arranged around the plate to add a decorative element.

Note: Dress the plates of frozen desserts at the very last minute so that the presentation is fresh looking.

Note : For more ideas on arranging and decorating frozen desserts on plates, consult the following volumes in this series "Prestige des Grands Chefs".
"Designer Desserts", (Philippe Durand)
"Decorating with a Paper Cone", (Alain Buys et Jean-Luc Decluzeau)

"Elodie" Sundae

Imagination is the key to making delicious sundaes. The creator is an artist, working with a palette of ingredients in a vast array of colors as well as flavors. To satisfy the various wishes of customers, a variety of toppings should be made fresh every day. The set up for making the sundaes should be very organized so that the sundaes can be prepared quickly. The "coupe" or container that is used, can vary according to the situation. Restaurants will present their sundaes differently than in an ice cream shop.

Making Ice Cream Sundaes

    Chocolate ice cream
    Strawberry sorbet
    Lemon sorbet
    Whipped cream
    Candied orange peel
    Candied lemon peel
    Strawberry (or raspberry) coulis

Serve with: Coconut tuiles

Ingredients

(recipes are in the last chapter)

Procedure

In a large goblet with wide base, place one scoop each of chocolate ice cream and strawberry and lemon sorbets.

Pipe a pretty rosette of whipped cream on top.

Place a few candied citrus peels around the sides and finish with the strawberry sauce ("coulis").

27

Sorbet Sundaes

These two sundaes, made with sorbet, are light enough to be served after a meal.

Mix a little of the sugar with the stabilizer. Stir together the apple juice, and the remaining sugar, stir well.

Whisk in the trimoline, stabilizer, lemon juice and Calvados. Cover and refrigerate several hours then churn in an ice cream maker. Firm, tart apples like Granny Smith are best for this dessert. Use 1/2 apple per person. Peel and slice, in a little water, dissolve 200 g (1 cup) sugar for every two pounds of apples. Add the peeled apples and cook over high heat a few minutes until softened but not mushy. Chill the cooked apples before serving. Blend the sugar and puréed apricot (the purée may need to be passed through a sieve.) Stir in the lemon juice, cover and refrigerate.

Ingredients *"Colombe" Sorbet Sundae*

This sundae is decorated with a cookie made in the shape of a dove which is "colombe" in French.

Cooked apples
Apple sorbet:
1 kg (2 lbs) apple juice
300 ml (10 fl oz) water
300 g (10 oz) sugar
75 g (2 1/2 oz) trimoline
5 g (1/6 oz) stabilizer
50-100 ml (4-8 tbls) Calvados
Juice of 1 lemon

Apricot coulis:
1 kg (2 lbs) apricot pulp
200 g (7 oz/1 cup) sugar
Juice of 2 lemons

Cookie shaped like a dove, made from almond «cornet» batter.
(See details chapter 6)

Champagne Sorbet Sundae

Mix a little of the sugar with the stabilizer. Combine the remaining sugar and water in a saucepana and bring to a simmer. Add the lemon zest and vanilla bean (cut in two down the center), cover and leave to infuse as the syrup cools. Add the champagne to the cooled syrup, whisk in the stabilizer and lemon juice. Cover and refrigerate several hours then churn in an ice cream maker. To lighten the sorbet in both texture and color, 50-100 g (1 2/3-3 1/3 oz) of Italian meringue can be added to the sorbet at the end of processing.

Bring the raspberry purée and sugar to a simmer, whisk in stabilizer if desired to thicken the sauce a little. Cool before using. Place two scoops of champagne sorbet in the bottom of a goblet. Add a few ripe raspberries. Pour a little champagne over the raspberries, then add some raspberry coulis.

Champagne sorbet	
1 L (1 qt) water	7.5 g (1/4 oz) stabilizer
1.1 kg (1 lb 4 oz) sugar	
Grated zest of 1 lemon	*Raspberry coulis*
Juice of 2 lemons	1 kg (2 bs) fresh or frozen
1/2 vanilla bean	raspberries
3 bottles of dry, good quality	200 g (1 cup) sugar
champagne	Juice of 2 lemons

These delicious little cookies can be filled with ice cream, sorbet or «parfait» and are easy and quick to prepare. They are traditionally served with Champagne or other chilled dessert wines.

Ingredients

150 g 95 oz) unsalted butter
35 g (1 1/6 oz) powdered sugar
100 g (3 1/2 oz) glucose
80 g (2 2/3 oz) flour
Pinch powdered ginger
Grated zest of 2-3 lemons
100 ml (3.5 fl oz) Cointreau

Ice Cream Filled "Cigarettes"

Procedure

Cream the butter, sugar and glucose, then stir in the remaining ingredients. Use baking sheets that are well buttered or lined with parchment paper. Pipe the batter in mounds and flatten with the back of a spoon. (Note: the batter can be made in advance and kept refrigerated several days. The batter hardens and can be formed into a sausage shape and cut into slices with a knife.) Bake at 200 C (400 F) until lightly browned.

While the cookies are still warm, mold them into cigarette shapes by wrapping them around the handle of a wooden spoon or the end of a sharpening steel (metal tubes are available for shaping these cookies.) They will harden as they cool.

These cookies are too hard to be served unfilled. Once filled with ice cream, the cookie softens a little and is easy to eat. They can be filled in advance and stored in the freezer in air-tight containers and served as needed.

Advice

This recipe is easy and quick to make but several precautions should be taken:

Watch the cookies as they bake; with a high sugar content, they will burn quickly.

Use a metal spatula to loosen the baked cookies from the baking sheet.

It is recommended to freeze the cookies before filling. The filling will not melt if piped into a cold cookie.

It is very practical to freeze the filled cookies on a cooling rack.

The rungs of the rack will keep the cigarettes from rolling around. Once frozen solid, store in an air-tight container.

The recommended serving is 3-5 filled cigarettes per person, but be prepared, your guests might want more of this delicious treat!

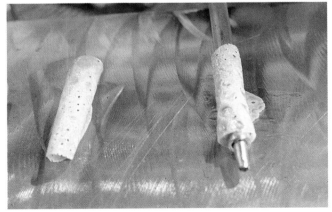

Ingredients

(For 50-60 small tulips)

Pistachio ice cream
1 L (1 qt) whole milk
250 ml (1 cup) heavy cream
250 g (8 oz) sugar
8 egg yolks (160 g (5 1/3 oz))
50 g (1 2/3 oz) trimoline
5 g (1/6 oz) stabilizer
100 g (3 1/2 oz) ground pistachio
Passion fruit sorbet
500 ml (2 cups) passion fruit juice
500 ml (2 cups) water
200 g (7 oz/1 cup) suagr
30 g (1 oz) trimoline

Raspberry sorbet
1 kg (2 lbs) raspberry seedless purée
400 ml (14 oz) water
350 g (12 oz) sugar
50 g (1 2/3 oz) trimoline
5 g (1/6 oz) stabilizer
Juice of 1 lemon
"Cornet" batter
500 g (1 lb) almond paste
3-4 egg whites

Pistachio Ice cream

Bring the milk to a boil with the cream, a little of the sugar, and the ground pistachio paste. Beat together the egg yolks, remaining sugar, stabilizer and trimoline.

Stir a little of the hot milk into the egg yolk mixture, then pour it all back into the pot with the milk. Return to medium heat and stir constantly as it cooks. The mixture should never boil, but to be pasteurized, needs to reach 85 C (185 F) for 3 minutes. Pour through a sieve and cool as quickly as possible over a bowl of ice. Cover and chill several hours then churn in an ice cream maker.

The ice cream is best if piped as soon as it is made.

Passion fruit sorbet

Mix all the ingredients, cover and chill several hours. Check the density (1147 D) and churn in an ice cream maker.

Raspberry sorbet

Mix about 30 g (1 oz) of sugar with the stabilizer. Mix all the remaining ingredients, whisk in the stabilizer then cover and chill for several hours to allow the flavors to develop. Verify the density (1147 D) and churn in an ice cream maker.

Tulip cookies

Break up the almond paste in a mixer and add the egg whites a little at a time to form a smooth, thick batter. Cut a round template from a piece of stiff plastic. Butter the baking sheets heavily and place in the freezer to harden the butter. With a spatula, spread the batter on the prepared baking sheets.

Harlequin Tulips

"Cornet" batter is shaped like a tulip for this dessert. Each portion contains three flavors of ice cream and sorbet that go well together. The challenge is to find three complimentary flavors in three contrasting colors. You might want to test the combinations before serving them to customers, some suggestions are listed below.

Three flavors provide the needed variety of color and taste but more than that would confuse the palate and detract from the experience.
This is but one use of the versatile almond "cornet" batter which is used to make "dove" cookies as well as ribbons and leaves for stunning presentations.

Possible flavor combination
Chocolate, lemon, strawberry

Pistachio, black currant, passion fruit. Chocolate, raspberry, passion fruit

Orange, chocolate, banana
Vanilla, chocolate, praline
Strawberry, honey, mint

Banana, cinnamon, chocolate
Pistachio, chocolate or black currant, pear

Bake at 180 C (350 F) until set and very lightly browned. Remove from the pan while still hot and mold into the tulip shapes using two soufflé dishes one larger than the other (or over the bottom of a glass with a small bowl.)

Order of procedure and assembly

Prepare the «cornet» batter, bake and form into tulip shapes.
Store in a cool, dry place until ready to use.
Prepare the ice cream and sorbet mixtures. Shortly before assembling the tulips, churn each in an ice cream maker.
Use a large piping bag with a large star tip. Fill the bag with the freshly prepared ice cream and sorbet, alternating the colors as shown.
Pipe beautiful rosettes into the tulips.
Place in the freezer until ready to serve. This dessert cannot be held in the freezer more than a few hours.

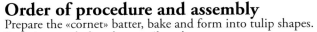

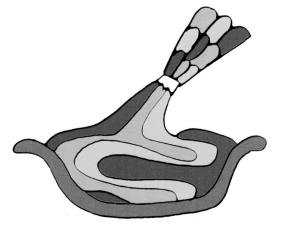

Ice Cream Filled "Tulips"

The «tulip» shaped cookies that make such an attractive edible bowl for ice cream or other chilled desserts can be made from «pâte à cornet» or «pâte à cigarette.» The batter is placed in circles on a well buttered baking sheet (or parchment-lined or non-stick.) The warm, freshly baked cookies are flexible, can be molded over the bottom of a glass or soufflé dish and become crisp and hold their shape when cooled. The tulip shape can also be molded out of nougatine.

The edible tulip-shaped bowl can hold several scoops of ice cream which can be garnished with poached fruits, whipped cream and other decorations. For an extra special treat, scoops of ice cream can be coated with chocolate to make frozen «truffles» which make an impressive addition to a tulip cookie.

Tulip cookies

Ingredients

For 12-18 tulips depending on the size

Pâte à cornet

250 g (8 oz) blanched almonds
200 g (7 oz, 1 cup) sugar
100-150 g (3-5) egg whites

Pâte à cigarettes

110 g (scant 4 oz) unsalted butter
130 g (4 1/3 oz) powdered sugar
3 egg whites
Few drops vanilla extract
130 g (4 1/2 oz) flour

Procedure

Pâte à cornet

Grind the almonds and sugar together to a fine powder.
Stir in the egg whites a little at a time. More egg white makes the batter thinner, more delicate once cooked but more fragile.

Pâte à cigarettes

Cream the butter and stir in the sugar.
Stir in the egg whites and vanilla then the flour.

Baking and forming the tulips

In France templates are sold for making perfectly round circles of batter as quickly as possible. The rounds can also be made by piping even-sized dollops of batter on the tray and smoothing them into a pancake shape with the back of a spoon. Use a non-stick baking sheet or one that is well buttered or covered with parchment paper.

Bake at 200 C (400 F) until light brown. Remove the warm cookies with a metal spatula and immediately form the tulips over the bottom of a glass or inside a small bowl.

The cooled tulips can be filled with scoops of ice cream and stored in air-tight containers in the freezer.

Ice cream truffles

Begin by making small, perfect scoops of ice cream and sorbet, placing them on a parchment-lined sheet and placing in the freezer to harden.

Next, covering chocolate is warmed to 45 C (about 125 F) which is a little hotter than for covering chocolate candies, then cooled until it is just warm to the touch. (This makes a more solid, but less shiny coating.) Dip the hardened scoops of ice cream into the melted chocolate with a quick motion so that the chocolate

shell is not too thick. Next roll each truffle in unsweetened cocoa powder and shake off the excess.

Immediately, place the finished truffles in an air-tight container and store in the freezer until ready to serve.

Variation

The tulips can be formed with circles of warm nougatine, which makes the dessert more rich in calories.

Whipped cream, fruit or custard sauces and pieces of poached fruits can be added to the tulip dessert.

The ice cream truffles can be stacked in a pyramid on a platter and also used to decorate ice cream cakes.

Any flavor of ice cream or sorbet can be used to make the tulip dessert. Choose colors and flavors that go well together. The amount and type of decoration will depend on the price or budget and the number of guests being served.

This is a perfect single serving of lemon sorbet. *"Citrons givrés"* can be made in advance and served as needed, offering a refreshing end to any meal and a healthy dose of Vitamin C.

Ingredients

(For 30-40 filled lemons)

2 kg (about 4 1/2 lbs) medium-sized lemons
(this will give about 1 L (1 qt) lemon juice)
1.5 L (6 cups) water

Syrup

1.2 kg (6 cups) sugar
100 g (3 1/2 oz) trimoline
100 g (3 1/2 oz) powdered glucose
20 g (2/3 oz) stabilizer (optional)

Cooked sugar (for decoration)

500 g (1 lb) sugar
150 g (5 oz) glucose
150 ml (5 fl oz) water

"Citrons givrés" (sorbet-filled lemons)

Procedure

Choose unblemished lemons with bright yellow color.

One liter (1 qt) lemon juice yields about 4 liters of sorbet.
The flavor can be enhanced by adding some freshly grated lemon zest to the mixture.

Sugar syrup :

Bring the water to a boil with the sugar (save a little for the stabilizer), trimoline and powdered glucose. Off the heat stir in the stabilizer (if using) mixed with a little sugar.

Cooked sugar :

Heat the sugar, glucose and water to 150 C (300 F) then cool to 130 C (275 F) to make the sugar decorations.

Order of assembly

Scrub the lemons well with a vegetable brush and rinse with cold water.

Cut off the top third of each lemon and scoop out the flesh.

Press the juice out of the lemon flesh. The white pith might add a bitter taste, so squeeze only enough to get the juice without crushing the pith too much. Strain the juice and measure 1 liter.

Cover and place the lemon shells in the freezer. Stir the cooled syrup to the juice and verify the density (1.120 D or 32 degrees.)

Churn the mixture then immediately pipe the soft, frozen mixture into the frozen lemon shells. Fill them quickly so that the sorbet does not melt and place in the freezer to harden.

Cook the sugar and glucose to 150 C (300 F) then cool to 130 C F (275 F), it thickens as it cools. To make the spun sugar, dip a fork or whisk with the tip of the wires cut into the cooked sugar and allow the liquid sugar to drop from the fork in long thin threads around the top of each lemon. The spun sugar can be stored for a short period in the freezer.

Harlequin Pineapple

This dessert gets its name from the traditional «harlequin» character in Italian theater who is always dressed in a suit covered in colorful triangular shapes. The colors of this dessert brings to mind the harlequin design.

Scoops of sorbet
and ice cream

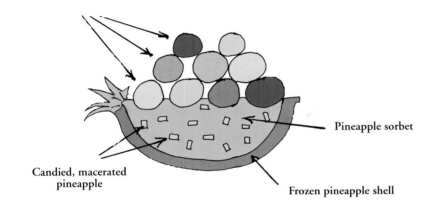

Pineapple sorbet

Candied, macerated
pineapple

Frozen pineapple shell

Ingredients

3 large, ripe pineapples

Pineapple sorbet
1 L (1 qt) pineapple juice
300 ml (10 fl oz) water
300 g (10 oz) sugar
50 g (1 2/3 oz) trimoline
3 g (1/10 oz) stabilizer
Juice of 1 lemon

Procedure

Prepare the pineapple
Choose very ripe, unblemished pineapples.
Scrub the outside of the pineapples and rinse
with cold water.
Cut them lengthwise in half, cutting neatly
through the leaves at the top.
Use the tip of a paring knife to cut out the
tough core in the center.
Cut around the edges and remove the flesh of

the pineapple, using a spoon to scrape the inside. Place the empty pineapple shells in the freezer.

Pineapple sorbet

Purée the pineapple pulp in a food processor. Strain the pulp through a conical sieve, pressing on the sieve to extract the maximum amount of juice.

Measure the juice and add more if needed. Mix a little sugar with the stabilizer (if using) and stir the remaining sugar along with the water into the fruit juice.

Strain and churn.

Cut two slices of candied pineapple for each serving. Cut each into dice and macerate in Kirsch.

Assembling the pineapples

Fill the frozen pineapple shells halfway with sorbet.

Cover the sorbet with diced and macerated candied pineapple.

Fill the pineapple to the top with sorbet. Cover and place in the freezer several hours.

Garnishing the pineapples

Place small scoops of pineapple sorbet and ice cream on top of the pineapple filled with sorbet and macerated fruit. Arrange the scoops in neat rows to look like the texture on the outside of the pineapple shell.

Nougatine «Cassolettes»

Individual servings of ice cream, sorbet or parfait served in a small nougatine cup or «cassolette» makes an impressive finale to an elegant meal. The nougatine cups can be made in advance and kept in an air tight container in a cool dry place, then filled to order with scoops of ice cream.

Ingredients
Nougatine
1.2 kg (2 lbs 8 oz) fondant
800 g (1 lb 10 oz) glucose
1 kg (2 lbs) sliced almonds
40 g (1 1/3 oz) unsalted butter
Filling (parfait)
Bombe mixture - Whipped cream
Grand Marnier

Procedure
Nougatine
This recipe containing fondant and glucose cooks evenly without constant surveillance. Use a heavy pot and cook over medium high heat and use a thermometer. Weigh the fondant and glucose and combine in a heavy saucepan. Cook over medium high heat to 180 C (360 F) and add the almonds. (The almonds do not need to be toasted because the heat of the sugar will cook them.) Remove from the heat and place the pot in a pan of cool water to stop the cooking. The sugar should be a light golden brown. Stir in the butter. To soften the nougatine for molding, place the pot in a warm oven (150 C (275 F)). If making in advance, pour the nougatine onto an oiled surface, wrap the flat disks and store in a cool dry place. Soften in a warm oven when ready to make the «cassolettes».

Forming the «cassolettes»
Roll out softened nougatine on an oiled surface with a lightly oiled rolling pin. (Special heat proof, non stick mats are available for the professional that can be used for rolling out the nougatine without oiling the surface.)

Cut circles of the nougatine with a round cutter and press into small, oiled molds. Cut the excess with scissors while the nougatine is still soft. Form a cover and adhere with hot caramel.

Filling the «cassolette»
Mix equal amounts of chilled bombe mixture and whipped cream. Flavor with Grand Marnier. Refer to the recipe for «Parfait Perigourdin». Freeze the parfait until firm enough to scoop. Forming the scoops of parfait. Cover baking sheets with parchment paper and place in the freezer. Form even scoops of frozen parfait and place in a single layer on the chilled baking sheets.
Cover and place immediately in the freezer to harden. Use as needed, placing the scoops in the nougatine cups just before serving.

Note: The scoops of parfait can be replaced with ice cream or sorbet molded in fruit forms. Decorate with cookie or marzipan «leaves». Use royal icing piped with a paper cone to add details to the presentation. Use several colors of sorbet/ice cream if possible.

«Cassolettes» with Profiteroles

This fancy dessert combines nougatine cups and profiteroles (cream puffs filled with ice cream, covered with chocolate.)

Making the «cassolette»
Refer to the recipe for «cassolettes» with Grand Marnier parfait. For this variation, make the nougatine containers in a «barquette» or «boat» shape to hold two profiteroles.

Profiteroles
Refer to Chapter 6 for the cream puff recipe («pâte à choux».) Make two cream puffs per person.
Prepare the ice cream, sorbet or parfait for the filling. If possible use two flavors and choose ones that go well with nougatine and chocolate sauce (Grand Marnier parfait, for example.)

Chocolate sauce
Refer to the recipe in Chapter 6. The sauce should be warm when poured over the profiteroles at the last minute.

Assembly
The profiteroles can be filled in advance and kept frozen.
For large groups the filled puffs can be placed in the nougatine containers and kept in the freezer until the chocolate sauce is added just before serving.

Tower of Ice Cream Centerpiece

This centerpiece of scoops of a wide variety of ice creams and sorbets is a stunning dessert to serve for any special occasion.
The colorful centerpiece can be mounted on a pedestal of sculpted ice and decorated with whipped cream and cookies in the form of doves to further enhance the presentation.

Ingredients

Scoops of ice cream and sorbet, choose at least 10 flavors in a variety of colors.
For example:

Chocolate	*Pistachio*
Praline	*Passion fruit*
Coconut	*Coffee*
Stawberry	*Apple*
Raspberry	*Mint*

Whipped cream
1 L (1 qt) heavy cream
150 g (5 oz/1 1/4 cups) powdered sugar
Chill the bowl and whisk in the freezer. Whip the cream to soft peaks in the chilled bowl, add the sugar and continue beating to firm peaks. Do not overbeat.

Procedure

Preparing the scoops of ice cream and sorbet

Place two baking sheets, lined with parchment, in the freezer.
Form large, even scoops and place them without touching on the chilled baking sheets. Cover and place in a sub zero freezer overnight to become very hard.

Almond cookie dove decorations

Make a template of a dove (or other simple shape) from a piece of stiff plastic.

Beat together until smooth, 500 g (1 lb) almond paste and 3-4 egg whites (enough for 2-3 dozen, depending on size). Butter several baking sheets and place in the freezer.

Spread the batter with a spatula over the template onto the buttered sheets.

Bake a few minutes (until set) in a hot (200 C (400 F)) convection oven.

Transfer the shapes to a cooling rack while still hot from the oven.

These cookies can be kept several weeks stored in an air tight container. This is a good item to have on hand for a last minute decoration or addition to a cookie tray.

Sculptures in ice

Ice sculptures can be made with blocks of ice molded in any size container.

Let the block of ice sit in its container out of the freezer several hours, so that fissures are not formed in the ice when the mold is submerged in warm water.

Professionals use a special saw made especially for sculpting ice, a regular saw can also be used to shape the ice.

Assembly of the centerpiece

Prepare the scoops of ice cream and sorbet and place on parchment-lined baking sheets in a sub zero freezer. Also place the metal cone used for forming the pyramid in the freezer.

Make the whipped cream. Line the metal cone with parchment paper which will facilitate the unmolding. Arrange a few scoops at the bottom, then pipe whipped cream along the scoops. Continue arranging the scoops, placing the next row between the scoops of the first. Vary the colors of each row for a pretty presentaiton. Continue with the rows of various ice cream and sorbet with whipped cream until you reach the top. Cover and place in the freezer several hours. Unmold and place the tower on a stand made of sculpted ice. Remove the parchment and decorate with the dove-shaped cookies.

47

Profiteroles Centerpiece

An individual portion of profiteroles is a mound of small cream puffs filled with vanilla ice cream and drizzled with chocolate sauce.

The concept translates very well to a large centerpiece as it resembles the classic «croquembouche» made with custard-filled puffs, the traditional «cake» for weddings, baptisms and communions in France. This is an elegant dessert for any occasion.

Ingredients

Cream puffs (for 60 puffs)
250 ml (1 cup) water
150 g (5 oz) unsalted butter
3 g (1/2 tsp) salt
200 g (7 oz) flour
5-6 eggs

Chocolate sauce
375 ml (3 cups) milk
125 ml (1 cup) heavy cream
100 g (3 1/2 oz) sugar
35 g (1 1/6 oz) glucose
475 g (scant pound) covering chocolate

Vanilla ice cream
1 L (1 qt) whole milk
250 ml (2 cups) heavy cream
1 vanilla bean, split
145g (4 2/3 oz) egg yolks
250 g (8 oz) sugar
30 g (1 oz) nonfat milk powder
50 g (1 2/3 oz) trimoline
5 g (1/6 oz) stabilizer

Procedure

Cream puffs

Bring the water to a boil with the butter and salt. Off the heat, add the flour all at once and stir to blend.

Beat in the eggs one at a time to make a smooth, thick batter. Pipe small mounds on lightly buttered baking sheets. Brush with egg glaze and sprinkle with chopped almonds, shake to remove excess, reglaze, sprinkle with coarse sugar. Bake at 180 C (375 F) until puffed and golden brown, about 15-20 minutes.

Vanilla ice cream

Dissolve the milk powder in a little of the milk.
Bring the remaining milk to a boil with the cream and the vanilla bean.
Add half of the sugar when the milk reaches about 20 C (about 80 F) then add the milk powder mixture when the milk reaches about 30 C (about 100 F).
Blend a little sugar with the stabilizer.

Beat the remaining sugar with the egg yolks.
Stir a little hot milk into the yolks, then add all the yolks back into the milk. Blend in the trimoline and stabilizer. Heat gently, stirring constantly, until the mixture reaches 85 C (185 F) and thickens slightly. Pour through a sieve and cool quickly over ice, stirring occasionally.

Chocolate sauce

Bring the milk and cream to a boil.
Off the heat, add the sugar, chocolate, glucose and butter. Stir until the chocolate is melted and the sugar is dissolved and the mixture is smooth.
Pour through a sieve and cool to room temperature.

Review of procedure for cream puffs

Make the cream puffs: mix the batter, pipe out even-sized mounds, brush with egg glaze, sprinkle with almonds, shake off excess almonds, reglaze over the almonds, sprinkle with coarse sugar. Bake at 180 C (375 F) until puffed. Important: if cream puffs are baked in a convection oven, reduce the air flow or pastries will puff too much and be too fragile for this dessert.
When completely cooled, fill the puffs with ice cream, place on baking sheets, cover and place in freezer several hours.

Assembling the centerpiece

Line the metal «croquembouche» cone with parchment paper. Place the mold in the freezer. Whip the cream ((150 g (5 oz)) powdered sugar for 1 L (1 qt) heavy cream). Transfer the cream to a piping bag with a #8 plain tip.
Begin by filling the tip of the cone with filled puffs.
Fill the cone with neat rows of puffs with the domed side out.
Cover and place in the freezer several hours.
Unmold onto a chilled platter, remove the paper and drizzle with chocolate sauce just before serving.

Frozen Crêpes with Bananas

Crêpes are a favorite snack in France, eaten with savory fillings for a light lunch or wrapped around sweet fillings for a sumptuous dessert. This versatile «wrap» can hold a hot soufflé or scoops of ice cream. Crêpe desserts are especially popular on restaurant menus.

Ingredients

One large crêpe per person
One banana per person

Banana sorbet
1 kg (2 lbs) banana pulp
300 ml (10 fl oz) water
350 g (12 oz) sugar
50 g (1 2/3 oz) trimoline
5 g (1/6 oz) stabilizer
Juice of 1 lemon

Raspberry sorbet
1 kg (2 lbs) seedless raspberry purée
500 ml (2 cups) water
450 g (2 1/4 cups) sugar
100 g (3 1/2 oz) trimoline
2.5 g (1/12 oz) stabilizer
Juice of 2 lemons

Chocolate sauce
750 ml (3 cups) milk
250 ml (1 cup) heavy cream
200 g (1 cup) sugar
75 g (2 1/2 oz) glucose
950 g (scant 2 lbs) semi sweet chocolate
50 g (1 2/3 oz) cocoa
75 g (2 1/2 oz) unsalted butter

Procedure

Banana sorbet

If using fresh bananas, poach them briefly to soften and keep the white color.
Mix a little sugar with the stabilizer (if using) and blend the remaining sugar and water with the bananas in the food processor.

Blend in the trimoline, stabilizer and lemon juice. Strain through a sieve, then cover and refrigerate several hours.

Raspberry sorbet
Blend the raspberry purée and water.
Mix a little sugar with the stabilizer (if using). Mix the remaining sugar into the purée, then the trimoline, stabilizer and finally the lemon juice.
Strain, then cover and refrigerate several hours before churning.

Chocolate sauce
Bring the milk and cream to a boil.
Off the heat, add the chocolate (chopped), sugar, glucose and cocoa. Stir until smooth. Stir in the butter and strain.
Cool slightly before pouring over the crêpes.
The sauce can be made in advance and warmed over a water bath.

Assembly
Sauté the bananas in a little unsalted butter (and sugar if needed.) Transfer the warm bananas to the crêpes, garnish with scoops of the two sorbets, coat with a little chocolate sauce and serve immediately.

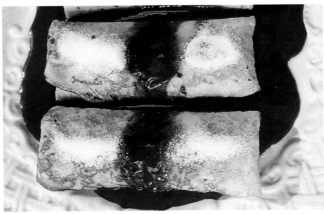

Arlette Goubier

Chapter 3 - Frozen Desserts

France

Frozen soufflé "Cardinale"

"Mignon"

« Le Sauvage »

"Délice au thé"

"Safari"

Rainbow

Ginger Mango

Frozen pear Charlotte

"Théâtre des Célestins"

"Pajamas"

"Le Périgourdin"

"France"

Ingredients representing the four corners of France make up this delicious and attractive frozen dessert.

- *Raspberries from the northeast.*
- *Apples from the northwest.*
- *Prunes in Cognac (or Armagnac) from the southwest.*
- *Lemons and apricots from the southeast.*

The mold chosen for this dessert represents the hexagonal shape of France. (France is sometimes referred to as «The Hexagon.») The top of the finished dessert can be decorated to pinpoint major cities or highlight a certain region. Notice that the mold is bottomless so that it can be easily lifted off the dessert.

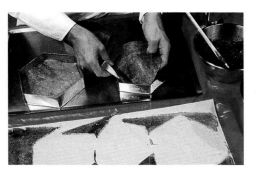

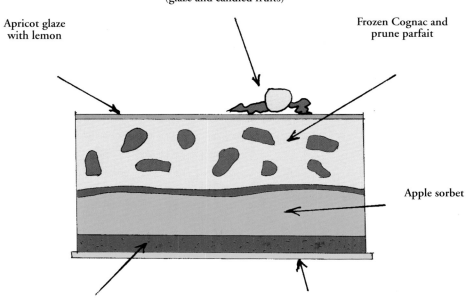

Decorations
(glaze and candied fruits)

Apricot glaze
with lemon

Frozen Cognac and
prune parfait

Apple sorbet

Raspberry sponge cake

Decorative base

Ingredients

(40 portions)

Raspberry sponge cake

(2 sheets 40 X 60 cm (16 X 24 in))

500 g (1 lb) seedless raspberry purée
300 g (10 oz) sugar
12 large eggs, separated
100 g (3 1/2 oz) pastry flour
150 g (5 oz) flour

Apple sorbet

1 kg (2 lbs) Granny Smith apples
300 g (10 oz) sugar
300 ml (10 fl oz) water
50 ml (1/4 cup) Calvados
Juice of 1 lemon

Frozen Cognac parfait

8 egg yolks
200 g (7 oz/1 cup) sugar
100 ml (3.5 fl oz) water
500 ml (2 cups) heavy cream
60 ml (2 fl oz) Cognac

Glaze

Apricot jam (strained)
Juice of 1-2 lemons

Garnish

500 g (1 lb) prunes macerated in Cognac

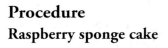

Procedure

Raspberry sponge cake

In a non reactive saucepan, simmer the raspberry purée with the sugar to 100 C (200 F.) Meanwhile, beat the egg whites to soft peaks.

With the mixer on medium speed, slowly pour the raspberry syrup over the egg whites.

Continue to beat until the meringue is cool. In another mixer, beat the egg yolks until thick and lemon-colored.

Meanwhile, sift the flours together.
Gently fold the beaten egg yolks into the raspberry meringue then fold in the flour.

Transfer the batter to parchment-lined baking sheets (this recipe makes 2-3 sheets 40 X 60 (16 X 24 in) depending on the thickness.)

Bake at 200 C (400 F) until springy to the touch but not browned.
Slide the cakes from the pans and leave to cool on the work surface.

Place the hexagonal molds on pans with parchment paper.

Cut pieces of cake to fit the shape of the molds and place in the bottom.

Apple sorbet

Peels and quarter the apples and poach in syrup (300 g each sugar and water) until soft, let cool in the syrup. Purée the poached fruit with the syrup until very smooth.

Stir in the Calvados and a little lemon juice.

Churn then spread in the bottom of the cake-lined molds.

Cover and place in the freezer.

Frozen Cognac parfait

To make the «bombe mixture,» which is the base of all French «parfaits,» combine 8 egg yolks and the sugar syrup in the top of a double boiler and whisk until thick and warm. Transfer to a mixer and beat at high speed until cooled.

Beat the cream to firm peaks, add the Cognac then fold into the cooled egg yolk mixture along with the macerated prunes.

Divide the mixture evenly between the molds and smooth the top of each layer. Cover and place in the freezer immediately.

Glazing and decorating

Stir a little sugar syrup and the lemon juice into the strained apricot jam to make a fluid glaze.

Brush the glaze over the surface of the frozen desserts and place in the freezer to harden the top.

Warm the sides of the mold with a blow torch and lift off the mold.

Use chocolate glaze piped with a paper cone and pieces of candied fruits to decorate the top like a map of France.

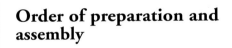

Order of preparation and assembly

Place the prepared cake in the base of the molds. Spread a smooth layer of sorbet over the cake, freeze to set.

Spread a smooth layer of Cognac and prune parfait over the sorbet, freeze to set.

Brush the top with apricot glaze and freeze to set.

Warm the molds with a blow torch and remove.

Decorate the top with lines representing rivers and towns.

Frozen Soufflé "Cardinal"

"Cardinal" is often used to name dishes that have a deep red or purplish color like the robes of the Cardinals in Rome. This frozen soufflé combines a black currant sorbet with a Kirsch-flavored parfait lightened with meringue containing pieces of macerated candied fruits. The creamy parfait is the perfect foil for the tart sorbet.

The dessert can be molded in a large rectangular mold for portioning into individual servings of any shape and size.

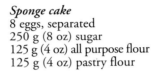
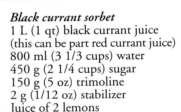

Sponge cake
8 eggs, separated
250 g (8 oz) sugar
125 g (4 oz) all purpose flour
125 g (4 oz) pastry flour

Black currant sorbet
1 L (1 qt) black currant juice
(this can be part red currant juice)
800 ml (3 1/3 cups) water
450 g (2 1/4 cups) sugar
150 g (5 oz) trimoline
2 g (1/12 oz) stabilizer
Juice of 2 lemons

Kirsch syrup
1/2 cup Kirsch
1 cup sugar syrup

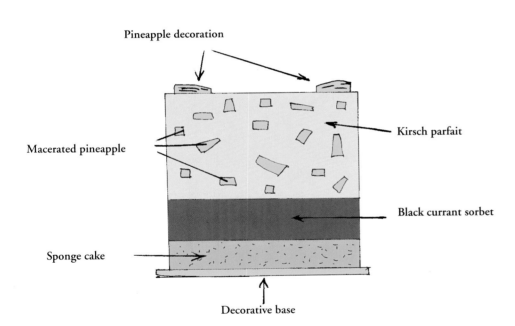

Pineapple decoration

Kirsch parfait

Macerated pineapple

Black currant sorbet

Sponge cake

Decorative base

Ingredients

(48 servings)

Soufflé mixture
Bombe mixture:
300 g (10 oz) egg yolks
400 g (14 oz/2 cups) sugar
150 ml (5 fl oz) water

1 L (1 qt) heavy cream
400 g (14 oz) candied pineapple,
   (diced and macerated)
125 ml (4 fl oz) Kirsch

Sprinkle powdered sugar on the piped batter which will forms pearls of sugar when baked.

Bake at 220 C (425 F) 5-10 minutes or until springy to the touch.

Slide the cakes off the hot baking sheets onto the work surface to cool.

Procedure

Sponge cake

Separate the eggs.

Beat the egg yolks with half the sugar until thick and light, set aside.

Sift the two flours together.

Beat the egg whites to soft peaks, add the

remaining sugar and beat to firm peaks.

Gently fold the egg yolks and flour into the beaten egg whites.

Pipe the batter in circles to fit the pastry rings on baking sheets lined with parchment paper.

This recipe makes about 12 cake circles.

Black currant sorbet

Mix a little of the sugar with the stabilizer.

Mix the remaining sugar with the black currant juice and water then whisk in the stabilizer, trimoline and lemon juice.

Strain the mixture, cover and refrigerate several hours.

The stabilizer (optional) thickens the mixture slightly and results in smoother texture and greater volume.

Candied pineapple

Choose unblemished pineapple slices.

Prepare a syrup with 1 L (1 qt) water and 500 g (1 lb) sugar (the density will be 1.1425 D.)

Simmer the pineapple until tender and cool in the syrup.

Transfer the pineapple slices to a low dish in a single layer.

Add enough sugar to the syrup to increase the density 2 degrees.

Bring the syrup to a simmer and pour over the pineapple.

When the syrup is cool, repeat the operation.

Place the candied pineapple slices in a wide-mouthed jar. Mix equal amounts of syrup and glucose, bring to a simmer and pour over the pineapple, cool then cover and refrigerate until ready to use.

Soufflé mixture

Separate the eggs, set the whites aside.

To make the bombe mixture base, lightly whisk the egg yolks. Meanwhile make a sugar syrup and when it has reached 120 C (250 F) pour it over the egg yolks with the mixer on medium speed. Continue beating until cooled. The bombe mixture can be kept several days in the refrigerator.

Next, beat the cream to firm peaks and fold it into the cooled bombe mixture. To lighten the parfait and turn it into a soufflé, make an Italian meringue with the egg whites and fold in with the cream.

Fold in the small dice of macerated pineapple and transfer to the molds immediately.

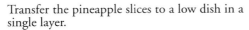

Order of preparation and assembly

Bake the cakes and place in the bottom of the molds.

Moisten the cakes with Kirsch syrup.

Pipe even layers of sorbet in each of the molds.

Add the soufflé mixture and smooth the top.

Cover and place in the freezer to set.

Heat the ring with a blow torch and remove.

Decorate the top with pieces of candied pineapple.

"Mignon"

This elegant yet easily prepared frozen dessert is best made when fresh raspberries are available.

Sponge cake, flavored with lemon zest, is used to line the mold. The center is filled with layers of raspberry sorbet and frozen raspberry mousse. A refreshing addition of fresh mint-flavored sugar between the layers brings out the natural acidity of the berries. The «Mignon» can be assembled in a tall pastry ring or in a large rectangular mold. The size and shape of the rectangular dessert makes it easier to customize the size of the portions which can be square, rectangular or triangular. Strips of sponge cake can be cut to fit and adhered to the sides of each portion with a little whipped cream. Champagne or sweet white wine would go well with this dessert.

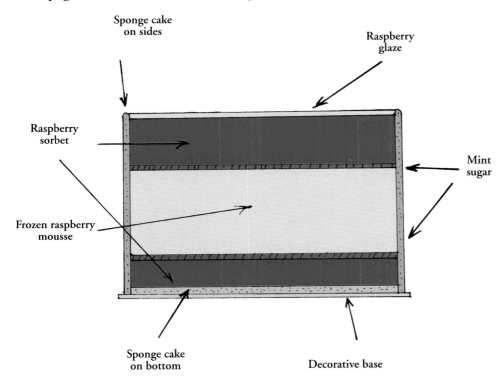

Sponge cake on sides

Raspberry glaze

Raspberry sorbet

Mint sugar

Frozen raspberry mousse

Sponge cake on bottom

Decorative base

Procedure

Sponge cake
Refer to the section on basic recipes in the back of the book.

Raspberry sorbet
Mix about 50 g (1/4 cup) sugar with the stabilizer. Mix the remaining ingredients together. Check the density (1147 D)

Whisk in the sugar/stabilizer mixture, stirring briskly to avoid lumps.
Cover and refrigerate several hours before churning.

Mint sugar
Chop the two ingredients together in a food processor, adding a little green food color if a deeper color is desired.

Ingredients

The following recipes yield 6 round desserts, 18 cm (7 in) in diameter, 5-6 cm (2 in) high.

Fresh Mint Sugar
200 g (7 oz/1 cup) sugar
30 g (1 oz) fresh mint leaves (cleaned and dried)

Raspberry Sorbet
1 kg (2 lbs) seedless raspberry purée
450 g (15 2/3 oz) sugar
.5 L (2 cups) water
60 g (2 oz) trimoline
5 g (1/6 oz) stabilizer
Juice of 1 lemon

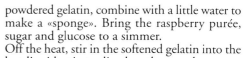

Frozen Raspberry Mousse

500 g (1 lb) seedless raspberry purée
1/2 L (2 cups) heavy cream
4 egg whites
250 g (8 oz) sugar

Prepare an Italian meringue. First dissolve the sugar in 100 ml (3.5 fl oz) water, then simmer until it reaches the soft ball stage or 115 C (240 F). Meanwhile, whisk the egg whites to soft peaks. With the mixer on medium speed, pour the hot sugar syrup in a steady stream into the

egg whites. Continue to beat the egg whites until cool.
Beat the cream in a cold bowl to firm peaks, cover and keep cold.
Whisk a little meringue into the raspberry purée, then fold this mixture into the remaining meringue.
Gently fold in the whipped cream. The mousse cannot be held in the refrigerator. Make it shortly before you plan to assemble the dessert, after the cake, mint sugar and sorbet are prepared. Transfer the mousse into the cake-lined mold (see assembly), cover and place in the freezer.

Raspberry Glaze

250 g (8 oz) seedless raspberry purée
250 g (8 oz) sugar
250 g (8 oz) glucose
2 leaves gelatin or
4 g (1 scant tsp) powdered gelatin
100 ml (3.5 fl oz) raspberry eau de vie

Soften the gelatin leaves in cold water. If using

powdered gelatin, combine with a little water to make a «sponge». Bring the raspberry purée, sugar and glucose to a simmer.
Off the heat, stir in the softened gelatin into the hot liquid, stir to dissolve, then cool at room temperature, stirring occasionally.
Stir the raspberry eau de vie into the cooled glaze.

Note: This glaze is used on top of a cake to add a shiny, mirror-like coating or as a layer inside a frozen dessert.

Assembling the "Mignon"

Place the metal ring in the freezer a few minutes. Cut a circle of sponge cake the same size as the ring and place it in the bottom.

Pipe a 1 cm (3/8 in) layer of freshly made raspberry sorbet on the cake, cover and place it in the freezer for 30 minutes.

Sprinkle an even layer of mint sugar over the sorbet. Spread a 3 cm (1 1/4 in) layer of freshly

prepared raspberry mousse, cover and freeze one hour.

Spread another even layer of the mint sugar over the hardened raspberry mousse.

Fill the mold to the top with sorbet, with a spatula dipped in hot water, smooth the top level with the top of the ring. Cover and place in freezer one hour.

Meanwhile, prepare the glaze.
Spread the glaze in a smooth even layer over the top of the dessert.

Heat the sides of the metal ring with a blow torch or hot towel and lift the ring straight up and off the dessert.

Cut a band of sponge cake to fit the side of the dessert and adhere it with a little whipped cream.

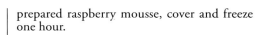

"Sauvage"

This colorful, frozen dessert combines the assertive flavors of passion fruit, black currant, cherry, bittersweet chocolate, pistachio and Grand Marnier in an unforgettable symphony on the plate as well as on the palate.
Each step requires careful preparation especially the black currant sponge cake which is moist and delicious if made properly.

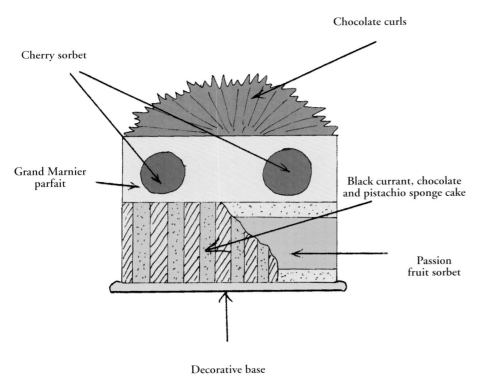

Chocolate curls

Cherry sorbet

Grand Marnier parfait

Black currant, chocolate and pistachio sponge cake

Passion fruit sorbet

Decorative base

Ingredients

60 portions : 10 round molds to serve 6 each or 30 small molds to serve 2. Each cake recipe makes 4 sheets 40 X 60 cm (16 X 24 in) to make multi-colored bands to line the molds.

Note: If passion fruit juice is not available, orange juice can be substituted.

Passion fruit sorbet

1 L (1 qt) passion fruit juice
700 g (1 lb 7 oz) sugar
100 g (3 1/2 oz) trimoline
100 g (3 1/2 oz) powdered glucose
5 g (1/6 oz) stabilizer

Grand Marnier parfait

Bombe mixture:
32 egg yolks
780 g (1 lb 9 1/2 oz) sugar
2 L (2 qt) heavy cream
200 ml (7 fl oz) Grand Marnier

Black currant sponge cake

750 ml (3 cups) black currant juice
400 g (14 oz/2 cups) sugar
16 eggs, separated
200 g (7 oz) potato starch
250 g (8 oz) flour

Chocolate sponge cake

16 eggs, separated
400 g (14 oz) sugar
200 g (7 oz) cocoa powder
200 g (7 oz) potato starch
100 g (3 1/2 oz) flour

Pistachio sponge cake

16 eggs separated
240 g (scant 8 oz) pistachio paste
350 g (12 oz) suagr
200 g (7 oz) potato starch
200 g (7 oz) flour

Cherry sorbet

2 L (2 qt) cherry juice
1 L (1 qt) water
120 g (scant 4 oz) powdered glucose
650 g (1 lb 5 oz) sugar
200 g (7 oz) trimoline

Procedure

Black currant sponge cake

Simmer the black currant juice and the sugar to 103 C (200 F.) Meanwhile beat the egg whites to soft peaks. With the mixer on medium speed, pour the hot syrup slowly into the egg whites. Beat until the meringue is cooled.

Combine the egg yolks, starch and flour and gently stir into the cooled meringue.
Spread the batter on 4 baking sheets lined with parchment paper and bake at 200-220 C (425 F) just until set to maintain the bright color.

Slide the cake off the baking sheet onto the work surface to cool.

Chocolate sponge cake

Beat the egg yolks with half the sugar until thick and light.

Meanwhile, beat the egg whites to firm peaks with the remaining sugar.

Sift together the flour, starch and cocoa.

Gently fold the egg yolks and flour mixture into the beaten egg whites. Spread the batter on baking sheets lined with parchment paper and bake at 200 C (400 F) about 5 minutes.

Pistachio sponge cake

Blend the egg yolks and pistachio paste until smooth, stir in the sifted starch and flour.

Beat the egg whites and sugar to firm peaks.

Gently fold the egg yolk mixture into the egg whites and spread on baking sheets lined with parchment paper.

Bake at 200 C (400 F) about 5 minutes.

Cherry sorbet

Whisk all the ingredients together.

Churn then form small even scoops of sorbet, place on a parchment lined sheet, cover and place in the freezer.

Note: The juice used here is from «griottes», a tart, bright red cherry.

Passion fruit sorbet

Mix the stabilizer with a little sugar, then blend all the ingredients.

Whisk the syrup and egg yolks together over a water bath until warm and thick. Set aside to cool, stir in the Grand Marnier.

Churn, then pipe an even layer of sorbet in the base of each cake-lined mold.

Grand Marnier parfait

Fold the whipped cream into the bombe mixture and transfer the parfait to the molds. Press the scoops of cherry sorbet into the parfait and place immediately in the freezer several hours.

Order of preparation and assembly

Stack the cooled cakes with seedless raspberry jam in between. Cover and place in the freezer to firm up so that neat bands of striped cake can be cut.

Arrange the bands of cake around the molds.

Pipe passion fruit sorbet in the bottom. Divide the parfait evenly among the molds then press the scoops of cherry sorbet into the parfait.

Decorate the top of the unmolded frozen desserts with chocolate curls.

Tea "Délice"

Tea-infused «parfait» and mandarine orange sorbet are combined in this exotic dessert. A decorative band of striped sponge cake with is used to line the mold for a spectacular presentation.

Choose a full flavored tea for a pronounced yet subtle taste.

The flavor and the texture of this dessert will not hold up for more than three to four days. Keep tightly wrapped and in a sub zero freezer.

To best compliment the subtle flavors of the Tea «Délice», serve it with Champagne, hot or iced tea or cold water.

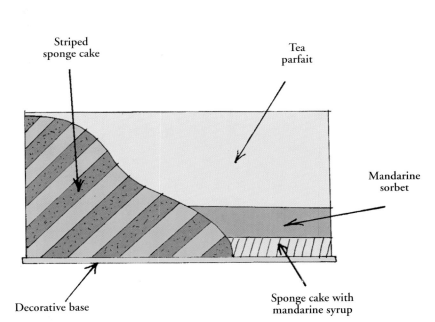

Striped sponge cake

Tea parfait

Mandarine sorbet

Decorative base

Sponge cake with mandarine syrup

Ingredients

Sponge cake

8 eggs
250 g (8 oz) sugar
125 g (4 oz) flour
125 g (4 oz) cornstarch
25 g (scant 1 oz) cocoa

This recipe will cover a sheet pan 40 X 60 cm (16 X 24 in).

This is enough sponge cake for 4 desserts, 18 cm (7 in) in diameter and 5 cm (2 in) high.
It is possible to make the sponge cake the day before. Cover it well with plastic wrap and store in the refrigerator.

Procedure

Sift the dry ingredients in two parts:
Sift together 70 g (2 1/3 oz) flour with 70 g (2 1/3 oz) cornstarch.
Sift together remaining flour and cornstarch and all the cocoa.
Separate the eggs. If the eggs are cold, warm the whites and the yolks to room temperature.
Beat the yolks with half of the sugar until very thick and lemon-colored.

Beat the egg whites with the remaining sugar to firm peaks.
To make the two cake batters, divide the beaten yolks and whites evenly into two bowls.

Gently stir, just enough to mix, the flour/cornstarch mixture into one bowl of the beaten yolks.

Carefully fold in one portion of the egg whites. Repeat the process with the cocoa mixture.
Transfer each batter to a piping bag and pipe out

10 ml (1/3 fl oz) liqueur; mandarine, cherry or ginger

Bring the water to a boil with the sugar.
Cool to room temperature.
Stir in the liqueur.

Mandarine Orange Sorbet

1 L (1 qt) mandarine orange juice
250 ml (8 fl oz) water
125 (4 oz) sugar
25 g (scant oz) trimoline (or honey)
2 g (1/12 oz) stabilizer
Juice of 1 lemon

Procedure
Bring the water to a boil with 100 g of the sugar
to make a syrup.
Cool to room temperature.
Stir in the mandarine orange and lemon juices
and the honey or trimoline.
Mix the remaining sugar with the stabilizer and
stir into the juice mixture, whisking constantly
to avoid lumps. Check the density.
Cover and leave in the refrigerator several hours

stripes of batter on the diagonal across the
parchment-lined, lightly buttered sheet pan as
shown. Also pipe four circles 16 cm (7 in) across.
Bake in a preheated oven 180-200 (400 F) about
five minutes or until the cake springs back when
touched lightly.

Mandarine Syrup

20 ml (2/3 fl oz) mandarine orange juice
200 ml (7 fl oz) water
200 g (7 oz/1 cup) sugar

for the flavors to develop.
Churn the sorbet in an ice cream maker.

Tea "Parfait"

15 g (1/2 oz) tea leaves
8 egg yolks (180 g (6 oz))
250 g (8 oz) sugar
1 L (1 qt) heavy cream

Procedure
Bring the milk to a boil.
Off the heat, add the tea leaves, and leave to

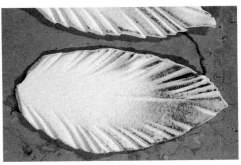

infuse. (Never boil the milk, the acidity from the tea will curdle the milk.)

Meanwhile, beat the sugar and egg yolks until very thick and lemon- colored.

Strain the milk through a sieve then pour the milk into the beaten egg yolks with the mixer on medium speed. Continue to beat until the mixture is cool.

Beat the heavy cream to firm peaks. Hold in the refrigerator until ready to assemble the dessert.

Order of steps for making the Tea Délice

Prepare the sponge cake batter and flavor half with cocoa.

Pipe the two batters in alternating stripes (with 8 mm (1/4 in) plain tip) on a sheet pan (40 X 60 cm (16 X 24 in)) and 4 rounds (18 cm (7 in)).

Bake in a very hot oven (180-200 C (400 F)) for about 5 minutes. (Quick baking at a high heat keeps the cake moist.)

Meanwhile, make the mandarin orange sorbet mixture and store in the refrigerator to allow the flavor to develop.

When the cake has cooled, flip it over and pull off the parchment paper.

Cut the sponge cake into strips 4.5 cm (1 3/4 in) wide. Line the sides of the molds with the cake.

Place the cake rounds into the bottom of the molds. Moisten the cakes in the bottom with the flavored sugar syrup.

Churn the sorbet mixture in an ice cream maker then pipe or spread a layer 1-1.5 cm (1/2 inch) in the bottom, cover and place in the freezer about 15 minutes.

Meanwhile, make the tea «parfait» and divide the mixture evenly between the four desserts and smooth the tops.

Cover and place immediately in a sub zero freezer for about 1 hour.

Unmold the desserts, by heating the metal rings with a blow torch then lifting the pastry ring off the dessert.

Cover and keep in the freezer until ready to display in a pastry shop or serve in a restaurant.

Decorate the top with a sugar paste flower and leaf.

"Safari"

The subtle sweetness of banana is treamed up with the tartness of passion fruit in this tropical dessert. The chocolate cake is moistened with sugar syrup flavored with passion fruit and ginger. It is recommended to let this frozen dessert sit in the refrigerator for about 1 hour before serving to soften it slightly to improve the texture as well as the flavor.

Assembling the "Safari" is relatively simple. Layers of the sponge cake are sandwiched with raspberry jam or currant jelly then cut into decorative bands. The top can be decorated with a dusting of cocoa powder or with a fancy design applied with a spray gun using a mixture of covering chocolate blended with cocoa butter.

Professional bakers may use a homogenized banana purée for this dessert. However, if fresh bananas are used, stir a little lemon juice into the bananas to keep them from browning which would detract from the appearance of the dessert.

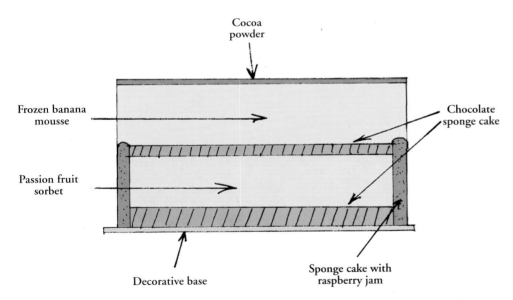

Cocoa powder

Frozen banana mousse

Chocolate sponge cake

Passion fruit sorbet

Sponge cake with raspberry jam

Decorative base

Ingredients

Sponge cake
8 eggs
250 g (8 oz) sugar
125 g (4 oz) flour
125 g (4 oz) potato starch
25 g (scant 1 oz) cocoa

This recipe will make two sheet pans 40 X 60 (16 X 24 in). This is enough for 3 «Safari» desserts measuring 16 cm (7 in) across and 8 cm (3 1/2 in) high.
Note: For the dessert shown in photos, you will also need 6 cake rounds the size of the mold requiring half of the following recipe.

Procedure

The sponge cake can be made a day in advance, covered and stored in the refrigerator or freezer.

Separate the eggs.
Beat the egg yolks with half the sugar until very thick and lemon colored.
In a mixer, beat the egg whites to firm peaks with the remaining sugar.

Meanwhile, sift the dry ingredients together (it may be necessary to sift twice to blend them completely.)
Gently stir the dry ingredients into the beaten egg yolks, just enough to mix.

Fold the egg whites into this mixture being careful not to deflate the batter.

Transfer to baking sheets lined with parchment paper.

Bake in a preheated oven (180-200 C (400 F)) about 5 minutes.

Passion Fruit Sorbet

500 ml (2 cups) passion fruit juice
500 ml (2 cups) water
200 g (7 oz/1 cup) sugar
30 g (1 oz) trimoline

Frozen Banana Mousse

500 g (1 lb) peeled bananas
(2 lbs with peels)
Juice of 2 lemons
4 egg whites
250 g (8 oz) sugar
500 ml (1 cup) heavy cream

Peel the bananas and purée in a food mill or food processor with the lemon juice.

Fold the banana purée into the meringue. Gently fold in the whipped cream.

With a spatula, transfer the banana mousse to the molds which have been lined with cake and filled part way with the passion fruit sorbet.

Smoth the top with a spatula, cover and place immediately into the freezer.

Procedure

Stir all the ingredients together until the sugar is dissolved. Cover and refrigerator several hours. Check the density (1147 D), then churn in an ice cream maker.

Procedure

Prepare the banana mousse after the other componants are made, because this mixture should be transferred directly to the cake-lined molds as soon as it is made.

First make an Italian meringue. In a mixer, beat the egg whites to soft peaks.

Flavored Sugar Syrup

200 ml (7 fl oz) passion fruit juice
200 ml (7 fl oz) water
200 g (7 oz/1 cup) sugar
10 ml (1/3 fl oz) ginger liqueur

Meanwhile, combine the sugar with 80 ml (1/3 cup) water, bring to a boil, then simmer until the mixture reaches 115 C (240 F/soft ball stage).

With the mixer on medium speed, slowly pour the hot syrup over the beaten egg whites.

Making the striped sponge cake

Make two chocolate sponge cakes on baking sheets lined with parchment paper.

Procedure

Bring the water to a boil with the sugar.

Cool to room temperature.

Continue to beat until the meringue is cool.

Beat the cream to firm peaks in chilled bowl, cover and refrigerate.

When they are cool, spread a thin, even layer of raspberry jam over the surface of one cake. Flip the second cake over on top of the first and pull off the parchment paper.

Stir in the fruit juice and liqueur, cover and refrigerate until ready to use.

Cut the cake in half. Spread jam on half and flip the other half on top. Pull the paper off the cake.

76

Place a baking sheet on top and press firmly to stick the layers together and make them as even as possible.

Place in the freezer to become firm before slicing.
Cut bands of the cake large enough to go half way up the sides of the mold.

Slice the bands into 5 mm (1/4 inch) pieces. Press these striped slices around the sides of the mold as shown.

Proceed with filling the mold as described above.

Rainbow

This dessert is not only easy to prepare in very little time, but it is economical as well. This is a lovely and delicious way to use the small amounts of ice cream that are left in the bottom of the containers. Half full containers not only take up room in the freezer, but a display case always looks better with full containers. It is usually made with four flavors in a variety of colors.

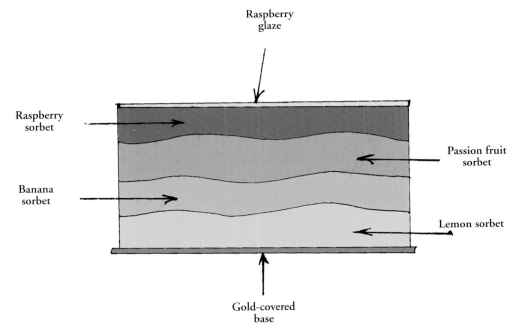

Raspberry glaze

Raspberry sorbet

Banana sorbet

Passion fruit sorbet

Lemon sorbet

Gold-covered base

Ingredients
(6 "Rainbows", 18 cm (7 in)across and 5 cm (2 inches) high))

Banana sorbet
1 kg (2 lbs) peeled bananas
400 ml (14 fl oz) water
350 g (12 oz) sugar
50 g 1 2/3 oz) trimoline
5 g (1/6 oz) stabilizer
Juice of 2 lemons

Lemon sorbet
250 ml (1 cup) lemon juice
1 L (1 qt) water
300 g (10 oz) sugar
50 g (1 2/3 oz) trimoline
5 g (1/6 oz) stabilizer

Passion fruit sorbet
500 ml (2 cups) passion fruit juice
500 ml (2 cups) water
200 g (1 cup) sugar
30 g (1 oz) trimoline

Raspberry sorbet
1 kg (2 lbs) raspberry purée
400 ml (14 fl oz) water
350 g (12 oz) sugar
50 g (1 2/3 oz) trimoline
5 g (1/6 oz) stabilizer
Juice of 1 lemon

Raspberry glaze
200 g (7 oz) raspberry purée
100 ml (3.5 fl oz) water
500 g (1 lb) apricot jam (strained)

Procedure

Lemon sorbet (1st layer)
Mix about 30 g (1 oz) sugar with the stabilizer, set aside.
Bring the water and remaining sugar to a boil and chill quickly over ice. Whisk the lemon juice, trimoline and stabilizer into the cooled syrup.
Cover and chill for several hours.

Verify the density (1147 D) and churn in an ice cream maker.

Banana sorbet (2nd layer)

Mix about 30 g (1 oz) of the sugar with the stabilizer, set aside.
Bring the water and remaining sugar to a boil and cool.
Add the lemon juice to the cooled syrup then place the bananas into the syrup as soon as they are peeled (this keeps them from browning.)
Purée the bananas with the syrup and press the purée through a sieve. Cover and chill several hours.
Churn in an ice cream maker.

79

Passion fruit sorbet (3rd layer)

Mix all the ingredients.
Cover and chill several hours.
Verify the density and churn in an ice cream maker.

Raspberry sorbet (4th layer)

Mix about 30 g (1 oz) of the sugar with the stabilizer.
Blend all the ingredients together.
Cover and refrigerate several hours.
Verify the density (1147 D) and churn in an ice cream maker.

Raspberry glaze

Note: French pastry shops use an apricot «jam» that is prestrained, with a high pectin and sugar content.
Place the starined jam in the mixer and on low speed, add the water and raspberry purée a little at a time to make a smooth sauce.
This sauce or «coulis» can also be used to pipe designs on a plate.

Order of procedure and assembly

Place an ice cream mold or stainless steel pastry ring in the freezer.

In order to pipe even layers, either use freshly processed ice creams and sorbets, or ones that have been slightly softened and stirred until smooth.

Warning: Do not let the ice creams get too soft. Lowering the temperature too much, could encourage bacterial growth.

Use a pastry bag with a large plain tip and pipe even layers of as many flavors as you wish — this will be a function of the size of the mold and the varieties that you have available.

The bottom layer should be one of the darkest in color and the firmest in texture.

Cover and place in the freezer a few minutes, while the next flavor is being placed in the pastry bag.

Serving the «Rainbow»

This colorful dessert is especially attractive when arranged on a plate.

Place slices of the «Rainbow» on plates and pour a fruit coulis or «crème anglaise» (custard sauce) on the plate.

Serve with cookies.

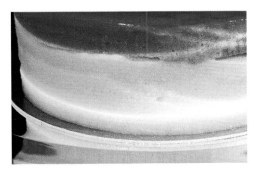

Smooth the top layer with a spatula dipped in hot water then pour on a smooth layer of glaze (the color of the top layer of ice cream/sorbet should look nice with the color of the glaze.)

Cover and place in a sub zero freezer for at least 1 hour before unmolding.
Heat the sides with a blow torch and slide the mold off.

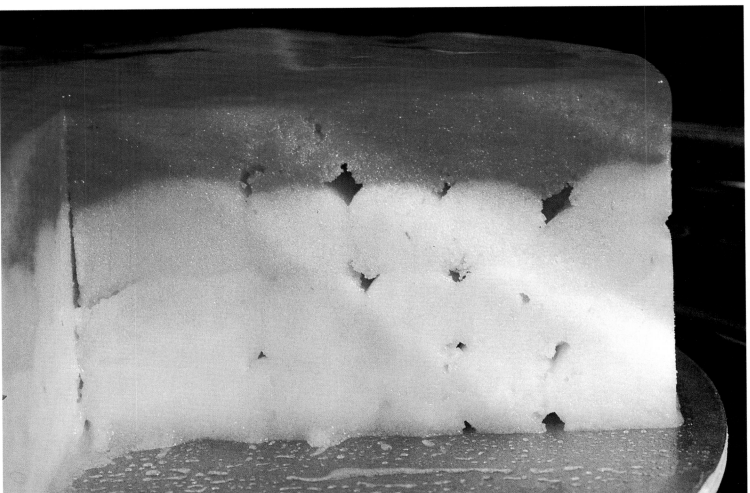

Ingredients

(For 5 desserts; 18 cm (7 in) wide and 8 cm
     (3 in) high
Pastry rings that are not high enough can be
wrapped with a collar of parchment paper is
secured with tape or string.

Almond/pistachio sponge cake
(Double this recipe to make 4 sheet pans
40 X 60 cm (16 X 24 inches) to make the sides
and cut out 10 circles 18 cm (7 inches).
450 g (15 2/3 oz) almond paste
6 eggs
80 g (2 2 3/ oz) ground pistachios
8 egg whites (250 ml (1 cup))
50 g (1 2/3 oz) sugar
60 g (2 oz) flour

Mango sorbet
1 kg (2 lbs) mango purée
300 g (10 oz) sugar
400 ml (14 fl oz) trimoline
5 g (1/6 oz) stabilizer
Juice of 2 lemons

Frozen raspberry mousse
500 g (1 lb) raspberry purée
500 ml (2 cups) heavy cream
4 egg whites
250 g (8 oz) sugar

Raspberry glaze
250 g (8 oz) sugar
250 g (8 oz) glucose or corn syrup
2 leaves gelatin (1/2 tsp powdered)
100 ml (3.5 fl oz) raspberry eau-de-vie

Ginger sugar syrup
200 ml (7 fl oz) water
200 g (7 oz/1 cup) sugar
10 ml (1/3 fl oz) ginger liqueur

Procedure

Almond/pistachio sponge cake

In a mixer, beat together until smooth the
almond paste, ground pistachios and the eggs.
In a separate mixer, beat the egg whites to firm
peaks, add the sugar to make a meringue.
Blend the flour into the almond paste mixture
then gently incorporate this into the beaten egg
whites.
Spread the batter on parchment paper-lined
baking sheets and bake in a preheated 190-200

Ginger-Mango

The exotic flavors combined in this frozen dessert are sure to please and the contrast of the golden mango sorbet and dark red raspberry glaze is attractive as well.
The mold is lined with an almond/pistachio sponge cake moistened with ginger-flavored syrup and layered with raspberry jam. The center is filled with mango sorbet and frozen raspberry mousse.

C (375-400 F) oven a few minutes until done. As soon as the cakes are out of the oven, slide them off the baking sheets onto a cooling rack to keep them from drying out.

Mango sorbet

Mix about 50 g (1/4 cup) sugar with the stabilizer, set aside. Blend the remaining ingredients together and verifiy the density (1147 D), add sugar or water if necessary. Add the stabilizer, whisking constantly so that no lumps are formed.
Cover and refrigerate several hours.
Churn the sorbet shortly before assembling the dessert.

Frozen raspberry mousse

Make an Italian meringue; dissolve the sugar in 100 ml (about 1/4 cup) water and cook over medium heat to the soft ball stage (115 C (240 F)). Meanwhile beat the egg whites to soft peaks in a mixer. With the mixer on medium speed, pour the hot sugar syrup into the egg whites, then continue to beat until completely cooled. Beat the cream to firm peaks and keep chilled. Gently incorporate the raspberry purée into the meringue, then carefully fold in the whipped cream. Transfer the mixture to the molds as soon as possible and place in the freezer.

Raspberry glaze

Combine the raspberry purée, sugar and glucose (or corn syrup) in a sauce pan and bring to a simmer. Soften the gelatin, then stir into the hot raspberry mixture and set aside to cool.
Stir in the raspberry eau-de-vie.
Note: This glaze can be used on top of a dessert or can provide a layer of a contrasting color inside a «bombe» or other frozen dessert.

Ginger-flavored syrup

Bring the sugar and water to a boil.
Cool over a bowl of ice. Stir in the liqueur.

Order of procedure and assembly

Place the metal rings in the freezer.
Make the almond pistachio sponge cake.
Use two layers to make the striped layers for the sides of the dessert. Spread raspberry jam on one of the cakes. Flip the other cake on top and pull off the paper. Cut the cake in half and spread jam on one half. Turn the other half over onto the jam, remove the paper. Repeat the procedure one more time, then place a baking sheet on top and press firmly to stick the layers together and even them out. Place cake in the freezer to become firm before slicing.

Cut the cake into bands approximately 4 cm (1 1/2 inches) wide (half the height of the mold.) Cut these bands into even 5 mm (1/4 inch) slices and press them around the sides of the molds.
Make the 10 circles needed for the base and interior of the desserts with the other two cakes.
Place a circle of cake in the bottom of each mold. Moisten the cake with ginger syrup.
Make the mango sorbet mixture, churn and pipe a layer (about 3.5 cm (scant 1 1/2 inches)

into the bottom of each of the cake-lined molds. Cover and place in the freezer.
Make the raspberry mousse. Place the second cake layer on top of the sorbet, moisten with sugar syrup then fill the molds with raspberry mousse. Smooth the top, cover and place in the freezer for about 1 hour. Make the raspberry glaze.
Coat the top of the desserts with the cooled glaze, spreading an even layer of the glaze with a spatula. Heat the rings with a blowtorch so that the rings lift off easily.

Frozen Pear Charlotte

The charlotte is a classic French dessert which can be prepared with a Bavarian cream or a frozen parfait. This stunning dessert combines chocolate and pears for a delicious marriage of flavors.

A band of delicate ladyfingers lines the mold which is filled with pear sorbet and chocolate ice cream. The top is garnished with poached pear slices and a pear sauce flavored with «Poire William» (pear eau-de-vie.)

Ingredients

(60 servings)

Pear sorbet
1.6 kg (about 3 lbs) peeled and trimmed pears
500 ml (2 cups) water
600 g (3 cups) sugar
20 ml (2/3 fl oz) lemon juice
60 ml (1/4 cup) Poire William
10 g (1/3 oz) stabilizer with 80 g (2 2/3 oz) sugar
300 g (10 oz) trimoline

Chocolate ice cream
3 L (3 qt) whole milk
625 ml (2 1/2 cups) heavy cream
28 egg yolks
600 g (1 lb 3 1/2 oz) sugar
200 g (7 oz) trimoline
10 g (1/3 oz) stabilizer
280 g (9 2/3 oz) bittersweet covering chocolate
180 g (6 oz) cocoa powder

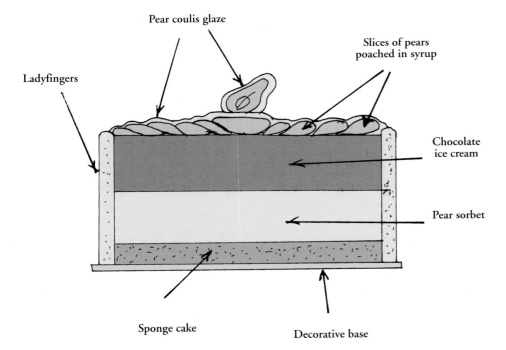

- Ladyfingers
- Pear coulis glaze
- Slices of pears poached in syrup
- Chocolate ice cream
- Pear sorbet
- Sponge cake
- Decorative base

Ladyfingers

Note: *The bands of ladyfingers can be piped any size to fit large molds (to serve 6-10) or individual molds.*

16 egg yolks with 100 g (3 1/2 oz) sugar
16 egg whites with 340 g (11 oz) sugar
320 g (scant 11 oz) all purpose flour
120 g (scant 4 oz) pastry flour

Procedure
Chocolate ice cream

Note: Use the freshest and best ingredients to achieve creamy, full-flavored results.

Make a crème anglaise: heat the milk and cream, whisk the egg yolks and sugar.

Stir the hot milk into the eggs, return to heat, stir until the custard coats a spoon, stir in the chocolate, cocoa and stabilizer (if using.)

Cool quickly over ice, cover and refrigerate overnight. Churn to a creamy consistency then transfer to the molds immediately.

Pear sorbet

Peel and trim the pears then poach in a syrup made with the sugar and water. When very tender, cool slightly then purée the fruit with the syrup until very smooth.

Combine the purée with the stabilizer mixed with sugar, pear eau-de-vie, lemon juice and trimoline.

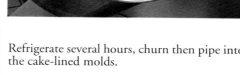

Refrigerate several hours, churn then pipe into the cake-lined molds.

Ladyfingers
Beat the egg yolks and sugar until light and thick.

Beat the egg whites and sugar to firm peaks.

Sift the two flours together.

Gently fold the egg yolks and flour into the meringue and pipe the batter in bands of «fingers» and circles on parchment-lined baking sheets. Sprinkle with powdered sugar and bake at 220 C (425 F).

Order of preparation and assembly

Cut the bands of cake in half and fit around the sides of the molds.

Place the circles of cake in the bottom and moisten the cakes with sugar syrup flavored with pear eau-de-vie.

Pipe the pear sorbet in even layers in the bottom,

freeze until firm then spread a layer of chocolate ice cream on top.

Cover and freeze until firm then decorate the top with slices of poached pears.

Pear «coulis» (sauce of puréed pears poached in syrup) can be poured on top or served on the side.

Théâtre des Célestins

This frozen dessert is a variation on another confection called the "Célestins", made of frozen parfait mixtures flavored with chocolate and coffee. The theater referred to in the name of this dessert is the opera of Lyon, a city where the gastronomy is world renown. The dessert is shown assembled in a large rectangle which is very practical for restaurant service. Portions of any size and shape can be cut to order.

The chocolate glaze that tops the "Théâtre des Célestins" can be made in large quantities and used to top other desserts as a sauce, for profiteroles, for example. The base of the dessert is coated in covering chocolate which hardens when cooled.

This moist, delicious dessert would go very well with champagne or other dry bubbling wine. Although the French usually have their coffee after dessert, an exception could be made here, as the flavor of the espresso would marry well with the coffee flavor of the dessert.

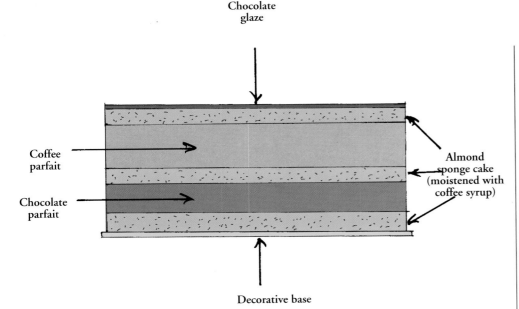

Chocolate glaze

Coffee parfait

Chocolate parfait

Almond sponge cake (moistened with coffee syrup)

Decorative base

Ingredients

Almond sponge cake

675 g (1 lb 6 oz) almond paste
9 eggs
12 egg whites (1 cup)
120 g (scant 4 oz) sugar
90 g (3 oz) flour

This recipe will make three sheet cakes 40 X 60 cm (16 X 24 in)

Chocolate parfait
4 egg yolks
125 g (4 oz) sugar
100 ml (3.5 fl oz) water
600 ml (10.5 fl oz) heavy cream
200 g (7 oz) bittersweet chocolate (chopped)

Coffee syrup
1 L (1 qt) strong coffee
600 g (3 cups) sugar

Procedure

Almond sponge cake

In a mixer at medium speed, beat together the almond paste and eggs until smooth.

In a separate bowl, beat the egg whites with the sugar to firm peaks.

Gently stir the flour into the almond paste mixture.

Gently fold in the egg whites and immediately transfer the batter to sheet pans covered with parchment paper.

Bake in a preheated oven 200 C (400 F) for about 5 minutes.

To keep the cakes from drying out, hold a corner of the parchment paper and pull cake off the hot sheet pans onto a cooling rack.

Coffe syrup
Procedure
Dissolve the sugar in the hot coffee, stirring from time to time as it cools.
Cover and refrigerate.

Chocolate parfait
Procedure
Cook the sugar and the water to the soft ball stage (115 C (240 F)).

Beat the egg yolks a little, then with the mixer on medium speed, pour the hot sugar syrup over the yolks. Continue to beat until the mixture is cool and thick.

Bring 100 ml (scant 1/2 cup) of the cream to a boil and add the chocolate. Stir the mixture until smooth.

When the chocolate «ganache» is cool, stir it into the egg yolks.

In a chilled bowl, beat the remaining cream to firm peaks and fold gently into the egg yolk mixture. Transfer to the mold immediately.

Coffee Parfait

Ingredients

4 egg yolks
125 g (4 oz) sugar
100 ml (3.5 fl oz) heavy cream
30 g (1 oz) instant coffee

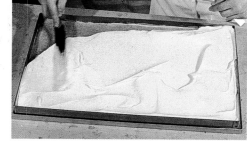

Procedure

Cook the sugar and the water to the soft ball stage (115 C (240 F)).

Beat the egg yolks a little, then with the mixer on medium speed, pour the hot sugar syrup slowly into the egg yolks.

Continue to beat until the mixture is cool and thick.

Dissolve the instant coffee in a little bit of the cream and stir into the egg yolk mixture.

In a chilled bowl, beat the remaining cream to firm peaks.

Gently fold the egg yolk mixture into the whipped cream. Transfer to the mold immediately.

Chocolate Glaze

Ingredients

800 ml (3 1/3 cups) heavy cream
500 g (1 lb) bittersweet chocolate
100 g (3 1/2 oz) glucose
100 g (3 1/2 oz) unsalted butter

Procedure

Chop the chocolate.

Bring the cream to a boil.

Off the heat, add the chocolate, glucose and butter.

Stir until the chocolate melts and the glaze is smooth and shiny.

Order of steps to make the "Théâtre des Célestins"

Prepare the sponge cake batter and bake on three sheet pans lined with parchment paper.

Prepare the coffee syrup.

Spread one sheet of cooled sponge cake with tempered covering chocolate, flip over on top of a sheet of parchment paper, and chill at least 10 minutes.

Place the metal rectagular mold around the chocolate-coated cake. Moisten the top of the cake with coffee syrup.

Prepare the chocolate parfait.

Note: The egg yolk and sugar syrup mixture (called a «pâte à bombe» in French) which is the base for a French «parfait» can be prepared for

this recipe in one batch then divided for the two flavors.

Transfer the chocolate parfait mixture to the mold, smooth the top.

Flip a second sheet of sponge cake over on top of the parfait, pull off the parchment paper and moisten well with syrup.

Cover and place in the freezer.

Prepare the coffee parfait mixture and place on top of the cake layer.

Smooth the top and place the last layer of cake on top, remove the paper and moisten with syrup.

Cover and place in the freezer about 1 hour.

Meanwhile make the chocolate glaze.

Spread the first layer of glaze on the cake (it should come right to the top), use a long, spatula to smooth the top, using the sides of the mold as a guide.

Place again in the freezer to harden.

Run a sharp knife around the edge and lift off the mold.

Warm the remaining glaze so that it is very fluid. Pour the second layer of the glaze evenly and tip and shake the cake a little so that the glaze completely covers in a thin coat.

« Pajamas »

With stripes like classic pajamas, this fanciful frozen dessert is a delight to look at as well as to eat, the perfect bedtime treat! The vanilla and raspberry filling is complimented by the pistachio, chocolate and vanilla sponge cakes.

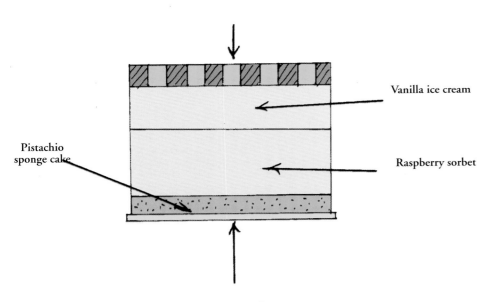

Vanilla/chocolate sponge cake

Vanilla ice cream

Pistachio sponge cake

Raspberry sorbet

Decorative base

Vanilla ice cream
3 L (3 qt) whole milk
4-5 vanilla beans
300 ml (10 fl oz) heavy cream
100 g (3 1/2 oz) non fat milk powder
24 egg yolks
700 g (3 1/2 cups) sugar
75 g (2 1/2 oz) powdered glucose
75 g (2 1/2 oz) trimoline
5 g (1/6 oz) stabilizer

Procedure
Sponge cake

Beat the egg yolks and sugar until thick. In another mixer, beat the egg whites and sugar to firm peaks.

Meanwhile sift the dry ingredients and divide in two parts.

Ingredients

«Vanilla and chocolate sponge cakes
32 egg yolks with 200 g (1 cup) sugar
32 egg whites (1 L (1qt)) with 720 g (scant 1 1/2 lbs) sugar
320 g (scant 11 oz) flour with 70 g (2 1/3 oz) cocoa powder
300 g (10 oz) flour with 100 g (3 1/2 oz) potato starch
1 tsp vanilla extract

Note: For the pistachio sponge cake, see recipe for «Le Sauvage.»

Raspberry sorbet
2 kg (4 lbs) seedless raspberry purée
720 g (1 lb 7 2/3 oz) sugar
1 L (1 qt) water
100 g (3 1/2 oz) trimoline
20 g (2/3 oz) stabilizer
Juice of 8 lemons

Divide the beaten egg yolks into two bowls and transfer half of the beaten egg whites to each bowl.

Gently fold in cocoa and flour into one bowl and incorporate the flour/cornstarch and vanilla into the other. For a golden color, a drop of yellow food color can be added to the vanilla batter.

Using two piping bags, pipe alternating strips of batter on parchment paper-lined baking sheets, as shown.

Bake at 220 C (425 F) without browning.
Slide the cakes off the pans onto the work surface using a corner of the parchment paper. If left on the hot baking sheets, the cakes will dry out and become brittle.

Vanilla ice cream

Slit the vanilla beans lengthwise. Combine the vanilla, milk, cream and milk powder, bring to a boil, cover and set aside to infuse 5 minutes.

Whisk the remaining ingredients together.

Whisk the warm milk into the egg yolk mixture, then return to medium heat and stir constantly as the custard thickens and heats to 85 C (185F.)

Strain and cool quickly over ice. Cover and refrigerate overnight.
Churn then transfer immediately to the mold.

Raspberry sorbet

Whisk all the ingredients together, cover and refrigerate several hours.
Churn then transfer to the mold.

Variation:

The raspberry sorbet can be replaced by pistachio ice cream.

Pistachio ice cream

Ingredients
3 L (3 qt) whole milk
300 ml (10 fl oz) heavy cream
100 g (3 1/2 oz) nonfat milk powder
250 g (8 oz) pistachio paste
24 egg yolks
650 g (3 1/4 cups) sugar
80 g (2 2/3 oz) powdered glucose
70 g (2 1/3 oz) trimoline
5 g (1/6 oz) stabilizer

Procedure
Bring the milk, cream, and milk powder to a boil, stir in the pistachio paste.

Whisk together the remaining ingredients, then whisk the hot milk into the egg yolk mixture. Stirring constantly, cook over medium heat until the custard thickens and reaches 85 C (185 F.)

Strain and cool quickly over ice. Cover and refrigerate overnight.

Churn then transfer to the molds.

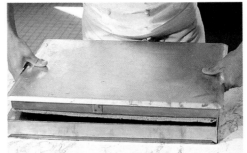

Order of preparation and assembly

Make the vanilla and chocolate sponge cake batters:

Beat the egg yolks and sugar in one bowl and the egg whites with sugar in another. Sift the dry ingredients. Divide the beaten egg yolks and whites and fold the cocoa/flour into one and the starch/flour into the other. Bake 220 C (425 F) 3-4 minutes (without browning.)

Slide the cakes off the baking sheet onto the work surface to cool.

Prepare the pistachio sponge cake.

Assembly:

The dessert is assembled upside down then inverted.

Slide the vanilla/chocolate sponge cake onto a baking sheet.

Moisten the cake with sugar syrup flavored with raspberry liqueur.

Spread an even layer of vanilla ice cream and smooth the surface.

Cover and freeze until firm. Churn the raspberry sorbet and spread over the ice cream and smooth the top.

Moisten the pistachio cake with syrup then invert over onto the sorbet, remove the parchment paper.

Brush a thin layer of melted covering chocolate on the cake base and place in the freezer several hours.

Place a baking sheet on top and invert the whole dessert.

Remove the parchment paper and metal form. Brush jelly glaze on the top and cut individual portions to order.

« Perigourdin »

In this full flavored dessert, inspired by the land of truffles, the truffles are made of chocolate. Raspberry, vanilla and Grand-Marnier marry well with the intense chocolate ganache.
This attractive dessert is relatively easy to assemble and can be served for any occasion.

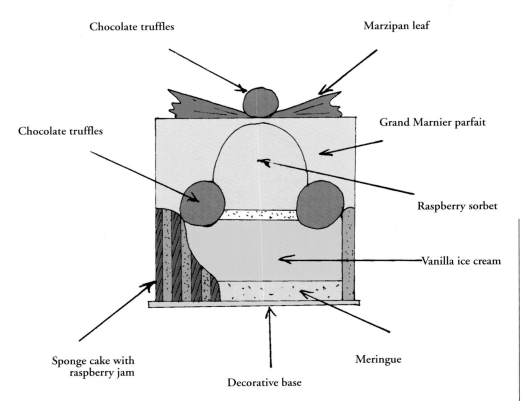

Chocolate truffles

Marzipan leaf

Chocolate truffles

Grand Marnier parfait

Raspberry sorbet

Vanilla ice cream

Sponge cake with raspberry jam

Decorative base

Meringue

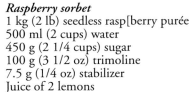

Raspberry sorbet
1 kg (2 lb) seedless rasp[berry purée
500 ml (2 cups) water
450 g (2 1/4 cups) sugar
100 g (3 1/2 oz) trimoline
7.5 g (1/4 oz) stabilizer
Juice of 2 lemons

Chocolate ganache
1 L (1 qt) heavy cream
1.3 kg (2 lb 10 oz) bittersweet chocolate

Grand Marnier parfait
Bombe mixture:
290 g (scant 10 oz/about 15) egg yolks
400 g (2 cups) sugar
150 ml (5 fl oz) water

Parfait:
Bombe mixture (above)
1 L (1 qt) heavy cream, whipped
250 ml (1 cup) Grand Marnier
Italian meringue made with 4 egg whites

Ingredients

Vanilla ice cream
1 L (1 qt) whole milk
250 ml (1 cup) heavy cream
8-10 egg yolks
250 g (8 oz) sugar
50-100 g (about 3 oz) trimoline
5 g (1/6 oz) stabilizer

Sponge cake
16 eggs, separated
500 g (1 lb) sugar
250 g (8 oz) all purpose flour
250 g (8 oz) pastry flour
(Make 1 1/2 times this recipe, use 3/4 for sheet cakes to make into striped bands, the rest for rounds of cake to fit the molds.)
Baked Swiss meringue
piped in rounds to fit base of molds

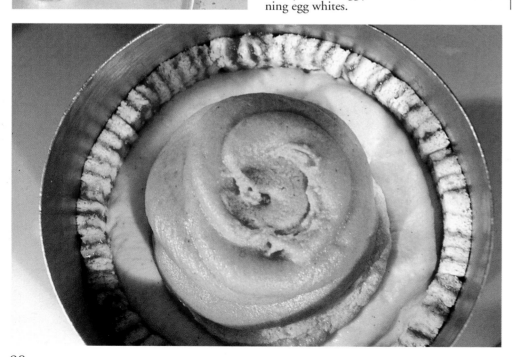

Procedure

Sponge cake

Separate the eggs.
Sift the two flours together.
Beat the yolks with the half the sugar until thick. Beat the egg whites to soft peaks, slowly add the remaining sugar and beat to firm peaks. Blend the flour into the yolks and lighten the mixture with a little beaten egg white.
Gently fold the egg yolk mixture into the remaining egg whites.

Line 4 baking sheets 40 X 60 cm (16 X 24 in) with parchment paper.

Spread the sponge cake batter on the baking sheets and bake at 220 C (425 F) 3-5 minutes. (Pipe the remaining batter into circles the size of the molds.)
Slide the cake off the hot baking sheets onto the work surface to cool quickly (it will dry out if left on the baking sheet.)

Sandwich the cakes together with seedless raspberry jam and place in the freezer to firm up before cutting into bands to line the molds.

The bands of cake shown for this dessert are 4 cm (1 1/2 inches.)

Vanilla ice cream

Bring the milk, cream and milk powder to a simmer with the vanilla bean (slit lengthwise), remove from heat, cover, set aside to infuse.
Mix a little of the sugar with the stabilizer.
Mix the remaining sugar with the egg yolks and whisk until thick and light.

Bring the milk back to a simmer, whisk a little hot milk into the egg yolks, then stir all the egg yolk mixture into the milk. Stir in the trimoline and stabilizer.
Return to medium heat and stir constantly as the custard thickens.
When the custard reaches 85 C (185 F) strain, cool quickly over ice.
Cover and refrigerate several hours before churning.

Raspberry sorbet

Blend the raspberry purée and water.

Mix a little sugar with the stabilizer and stir the remaining sugar into the fruit purée.

Stir in the trimoline, then the stabilizer and lemon juice.

Strain, cover and refrigerate several hours before churning.

Chocolate ganache truffles

Chop the chocolate into small pieces.
Bring the cream to a boil, remove from the heat, add the chocolate.
Cool until firm. Pipe out the truffles with a piping bag.
Roll the truffles into a ball, dip in melted covering chocolate and dust with cocoa powder.

Grand Marnier parfait

Bombe mixture:
Whisk the egg yolks in a mixer. Meanwhile cook the sugar and water to 120 C (250 F.)
With the mixer on medium speed, gradually pour the hot syrup into the egg yolks, continue beating until the mixture is cool.
The bombe mixture must be completely cooled before blending with the whipped cream.
The bombe mixture can be made in advance in large quantities and stored in covered containers in the freezer.

Parfait:
Whip the cream in a chilled bowl.
Stir the Grand Marnier into the bombe mixture.
Stir a little of the whipped cream into the bombe mixture, then gently fold it back into the cream. The parfait should not be liquid, but light and mousse-like in texture.
A little Italian meringue can be folded into the parfait to lighten it.

Order of preparation and assembly

Place the metal forms on a sheet lined with parchment paper.

Cut bands of cake layered with raspberry jam as shown and place around the sides of the metal forms.
Place the baked meringues in the bottom of the molds.
Churn the vanilla ice cream and spread an even layer over the meringue.
Place the sponge cake rounds on the ice cream and moisten with sugar syrup flavored with Grand Marnier.
Churn the raspberry sorbet and spread a layer with a domed center.

Place the chocolate truffles around the edge.
Cover and place in the freezer.
Meanwhile, prepare the Grand Marnier parfait and cover the sorbet and truffles with this mixture, smooth the top.
Cover and place in freezer several hours.
Heat the metal form with a blow torch and remove.

Decorate the top with truffles and green marzipan leaves. Use the blow torch to add a brown contrast to the leaves.

Arlette Goubier

Chapter 4 - Frozen Log-shaped Cakes ("bûches")

"La bûche Ardéchoise"

Hawaiian log cake

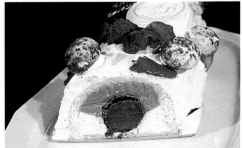

"La bûche Périgourdine"

Baked Alaska "St. Sylvestre"

Troïka

"La bûche Dorothée"

Frozen Nougat

Log Cake («Bûche) «Archédoise»

Candied chestnuts are one of the treats that the French enjoy during the Christmas holidays. This traditional «bûche» or log-shaped cake made with ice cream and candied chestnuts is an ideal dessert following Christmas dinner.
The best chestnuts in France come from the southwest Ardèche region, which gives this dessert its name.
Frozen desserts in this cylindrical shape have become more popular over the years, because they are so easy to slice and serve.

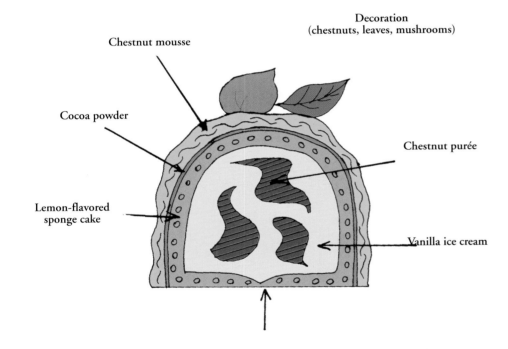

Decoration
(chestnuts, leaves, mushrooms)

Chestnut mousse

Cocoa powder

Chestnut purée

Lemon-flavored sponge cake

Vanilla ice cream

Decorative base

Ingredients

Enough for 3 log cakes 50 cm (20 in) long and 6-7 cm (2 3/4 in) high.

Vanilla ice cream
(Double this recipe to make 4 sheet pans 40 X 60 cm (16 X 24 inches) to make the sides and cut out 10 circles 18 cm (7 inches).

Sponge cake
(for one sheet pan 40 X 60 cm (16 X 24 in)

4 eggs
125 g (4 oz) sugar
75 g (2 1/2 oz) flour
75 g (2 1/2 oz) cornstarch
Grated zest of 1 lemon

Chestnut mousse
100 g (3 1/2 oz) «bombe» mixture
(see chocolate parfait/»Théâtre des Célestins))
1 L (1 qt) heavy cream
300 g (10 oz) sweetened chestnut purée

Decorations, for each log cake:
2 candied chestnuts
3 meringue mushrooms
2 cookie leaves
1 small plastic pine tree (optional)
Cocoa powder

Procedure
Vanilla ice cream

Bring the milk and cream to a simmer with the vanilla bean (split down the center) and a little bit of the sugar.

Beat the egg yolks until thick and lemon-colored with the remaining sugar, trimoline and stabilizer.

Whisk a little of the hot milk into the yolks, then whisk all the egg yolk mixture into the hot milk.

Over medium low heat, stirring constantly, cook until the mixture reaches 85 C (185 F) and maintain this temperature for 3 minutes (this procedure pasturizes the custard.)

Pour through a sieve, cool quickly over a bowl of ice (stirring occasionally.)

Churn the mixture, adding the chestnut purée by spoonfuls when the ice cream is almost set

to achieve a marbled affect.
Transfer the ice cream to the molds immediately.

Sponge cake

Separate the eggs. Beat the egg yolks and half of the sugar until thick and lemon-colored.

Beat the egg whites to soft peaks, add the remaining sugar and beat to firm peaks.

Sift the flour and cornstarch together, stir the grated lemon zest into the flour.

Stir the flour into the beaten egg yolks, just enough to mix.

Gently incorporate the beaten egg whites and spread the batter on a parchment paper-lined baking sheet.

Bake in a 180-200 C (375-400 F) preheated oven about 5 minutes or until springy to the touch. Slide the cake off the baking sheet to cool quickly.

Chestnut mousse

In a chilled bowl, beat the cream to firm peaks. Fold the «bombe» mixture into the chestnut purée.

Gently incorporate the whipped cream into the the chestnut mixture.

Place in the mold as soon as possible.

Order of procedure and assembly

Cut the cooled sponge cake into three strips and line the log-shaped molds.

Make the vanilla ice cream with chestnut purée and use a piping bag with a large opening to fill each mold.

Fold the ends of the cake over the ice cream, cover and place in the freezer for about 1 hour. Prepare the chestnut mousse.

Unmold the bûche onto a decorative base and spread the freshly prepared mousse over the outside of each bûche, using the spatual to form «bark» and «sawed off branches» of the log.

Decorate with candied chestnuts and meringue mushrooms.

Just before serving, sprinkle with cocoa powder.

This not only makes the log look very pretty, but the cocoa flavor brings out the taste of the chestnuts.

Hawaiian Log Cake

This log-shaped cake is easy to assemble and is ideal for dessert on a hot evening. The combination of pineapple sorbet, coconut ice cream and Kirsch parfait is very refreshing. The candied pineapple described in the recipe can be replaced with fresh or poached pineapple macerated in liqueur. «Bûches» or log-shaped cakes are very practical for serving a large group or for service in a restaurant. Each slice looks very attractive and the plate can be decorated to augment the presentation.

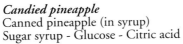

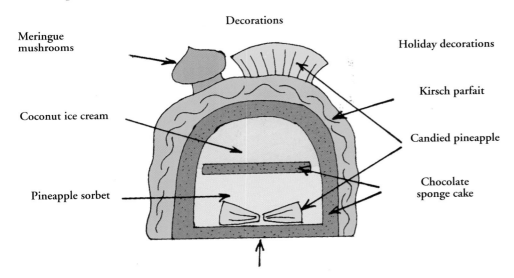

Decorations

Meringue mushrooms

Holiday decorations

Coconut ice cream

Kirsch parfait

Candied pineapple

Chocolate sponge cake

Pineapple sorbet

Decorative base

Ingredients

(Three log cakes)

Chocolate sponge cake
(4 cakes 40 X 60 cm (16 X 24 in))
16 eggs
500 g (1 lb) sugar
200 g (7 oz) pastry flour
200 g (7 oz) all purpose flour
100 g (3 1/2 oz) cocoa powder

Pineapple sorbet
1 L (qt) pineapple juice
250 ml (1 cup) water
300 g (10 oz) sugar
50 g (1 2/3 oz) trimoline
3 g (1/12 oz) stabilizer
Juice of 1 lemon

Coconut ice cream
1 L (1 qt) whole milk
1 L (1 qt) coconut milk
125 g (4 oz) non fat milk powder
300 ml (10 fl oz) heavy cream
470 g (scant 1 lb) sugar
100 g (3 1/2 oz) dextrose
15 g (1/2 oz) stabilizer

Kirsch Parfait
Bombe mixture made with 15 yolks
(see «Perigourdin»)
1 L (1 qt) heavy cream
250 ml (1 cup) Kirsch

Parfait Mixture for Decoration
Whipped cream flavored with Kirsch
Bombe mixture to taste

Candied pineapple
Canned pineapple (in syrup)
Sugar syrup - Glucose - Citric acid

Procedure

Chocolate sponge cake
Separate the eggs and beat the yolks with half the sugar until thick.
Sift the flour and cocoa together.
Whisk the egg whites to soft peaks then slowly add the remaining sugar at medium speed and beat until firm peaks are formed.

107

Stir the flour/cocoa into the beaten egg yolks. Stir a little of the beaten egg whites into the mixture to lighten it. Gently fold the lightened egg yolk mixture into the remaining egg whites. Spread the batter on four sheet pans lined with parchment paper and bake 3-5 minutes at 220 C (435 F.). Slide the cakes off the hot baking sheets onto the work surface to cool.

Pineapple sorbet

To make fresh pineapple juice, cut off the skin and remove the tough center portion. Extract the juice in a machine made for that purpose and strain it. Mix a little of the sugar with the stabilizer. Mix the pineapple juice with the remaining sugar, water and trimoline.

Whisk in the stabilizer and lemon juice, cover and refrigerate several hours.

Pour through a strainer and churn just before assembling the dessert.

Coconut ice cream

Bring the milk, coconut milk and cream to a simmer. Stir in the milk powder, dextrose and a little of the sugar.

Mix the remaining sugar with the stabilizer. Cook over medium heat, stirring constantly until the mixture reaches 85 C (185 F), strain then cool quickly over ice.

Cover and refrigerate several hours, strain then churn shortly before assembling the dessert.

Kirsch parfait

Whip the cream to firm peaks.

Gently fold in the bombe mixture and Kirsch. The parfait mixture should be like mousse in texture and not too liquid.

Candied pineapple

Candied pineapple is used in this frozen dessert

because the high sugar content keeps it from freezing. Fresh or poached fruit becomes too icy. Another alternative is to macerate poached fruit in liqueur. Candied pineapple can be prepared with fresh pineapple, but using good quality canned pineapple in syrup eliminates the first step. Choose thick slices about the same size. Make a sugar syrup with 1 L (1 qt) water and 600 g (3 cups) sugar.

Arrange the poached pineapple slices in a single layer in a non reactive, heat proof dish.

Bring the syrup to a boil and pour it over the pineapple, cover and refrigerate overnight.

Drain off the syrup and check its density. Add enough sugar to raise the density by 2 degrees. Bring the syrup back to a boil, pour over the pineapple slices, cover and leave to cool.

Repeat this process until the pineapple is candied, making enough new syrup each time to completely cover the fruit.

To preserve the candied pineapple, blend the heavy syrup from the last operation with half its weight in glucose. Arrange the slices in a glass jar. Bring the syrup with glucose to a boil, pour over the fruit, cool, then cover and refrigerate.

Preparation and assembly

To facilitate lining the mold with the cake:

Cut a strip of parchment paper the width of the mold and longer than the mold. Cut the paper into thirds. Cut the cake to fit the paper, moisten with flavored sugar syrup. Place one strip in the bottom first, then place remaining strips along the sides. Once the molds are lined with moistened sponge cake, churn the sorbet and pipe even layers to cover the cake, smooth the surface. Place a rectangle of cake on the sorbet, moisten with syrup, cover and place in the freezer to become firm.

Cut the candied pineapple into small pieces and spread in even layers on the cake.

Churn the coconut ice cream and divide evenly between the molds, smooth the top, cover and freeze several hours. Heat the mold with a blow torch to remove it easily.

Trim the ends of the cake and place on top of the «log» to make sawed off «branches.»

Prepare the parfait, pipe the mixture with a flat tip over the surface of the cake. Smooth the ends with a spatula. Freeze until firm then decorate with chocolate piped with a paper cone and place meringue mushrooms on top.

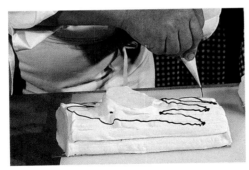
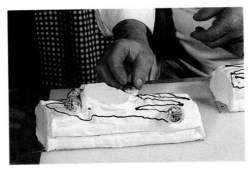

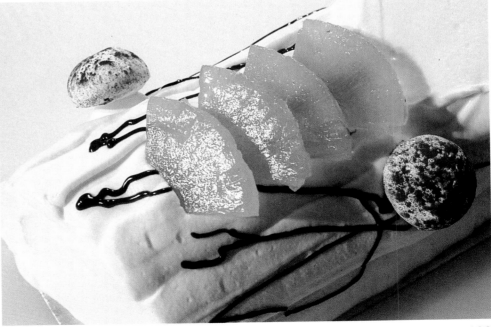

109

«La Bûche Périgourdine»

This log cake made with truffles takes its name from the southwest region of France famous for black truffles found in the oak forests of Périgord. The log shape also evokes the woods of the region.
Chocolate combined with raspberry and Grand Marnier is sure to please your guests.

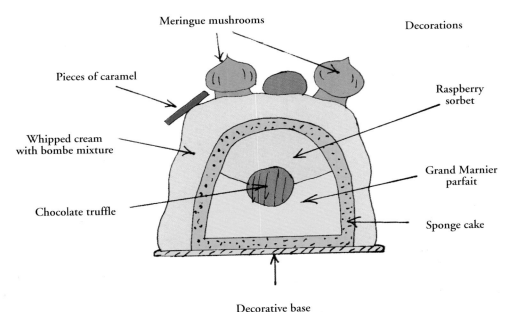

- Meringue mushrooms
- Decorations
- Pieces of caramel
- Raspberry sorbet
- Whipped cream with bombe mixture
- Grand Marnier parfait
- Chocolate truffle
- Sponge cake
- Decorative base

Ingredients

Sponge cake
(4 sheet pans 40 X 60 cm (16 X 24 in))
16 large eggs
500 g (1 lb) sugar
250 g (8 oz) all pupose flour
250 g (8 oz) pastry flour

Raspberry sorbet
1 kg (2 lbs) seedless raspberry purée
500 ml (2 cups) water
450 g (2 1/3 cups) sugar
100 g (3 1/2 oz) trimoline
7.5 g (1/4 oz) stabilizer
Juice of 2 lemons

Grand Marnier parfait
Bombe mixture:
580 g (1 lb 2 2/3 oz/about 30) egg yolks
800 g (4 cups) sugar
300 ml (10 fl oz) water

Parfait:
Half of bombe recipe
(reserve rest for the outside of log cake)
1 L (1 qt) whipped cream
250 ml (1 cup) Grand Marnier

Parfait for outside of cake
Bombe mixture
Whipped cream (to taste)

Chocolate truffles
1 L (1 qt) heavy cream
1.3 kg (1 lb 10 oz) bittersweet chocolate

Procedure

Sponge cake
Separate the eggs.
Beat the yolks with half of the sugar until light and thick.
Sift the two flours together.
Beat the egg whites to soft peaks, gradually add the sugar and beat to firm peaks.
Mix the flour into the egg yolks, stir in a little egg white to lighten.
Gently fold the egg yolks into the egg whites.
Spread the batter on the baking sheets lined with parchment paper and bake at 220 C (425F) about 3-5 minutes.

Fold the chilled bombe mixture into the whipped cream (and meringue), then gently stir in the Grand Marnier without deflating the mixture (it should remain very light.)

Light cream for the outside of the «bûche»

Combine whipped cream with less bombe mixture than for the parfait. Flavor with a little Grand Marnier.

Raspberry sorbet

Mix the raspberry purée and the water.
Mix a little sugar with the stabilizer.
Blend the sugar, trimoline into the purée, then the stabilizer and lemon juice.
Strain, cover and refrigerate several hours before churning.

Grand Marnier parfait

Bombe mixture:
Simmer the sugar and water to 120 C (250 F.)
Meanwhile, beat the egg yolks in a mixer until frothy.
With the mixer on medium speed, slowly pour the syrup into the eggs and continue beating until the mixture cools.
Chill the mixture before folding in the whipped cream.
Bombe mixture can be made in advance and kept in the refrigerator or freezer.

Parfait:
Beat the cream to firm peaks in a chilled bowl.
If a lighter parfait is desired, make an Italian meringue with 4 egg whites.

Chocolate truffles

Chop the chocolate into smalll pieces.
Bring the cream to a boil, remove from heat and add the chocolate.
Chill, then pipe the truffle mixture into even mounds on a parchment-lined sheet.
Roll into balls, coat in melted covering chocolate and dust with cocoa powder.

Order of preparation and assembly

To facilitate the lining of the molds, cut strips of parchment paper a little longer than the mold. Cut three strips of cake to fit and place the strips one at a time into the mold.
Moisten the cake with sugar syrup flavored with Grand Marnier.
Churn the raspberry sorber then pipe an even layer on top of the cake, smooth the surface, place the truffles on top, place in freezer.
Prepare the Grand Marnier parfait, cover the sorbet and truffles.
Cut a rectangle of cake for the base, moisten with syrup, cover and place in freezer several hours.
To remove the mold, heat it with a blow torch. Trim the ends and use these pieces of cake to make the sawed off «branches» on top.
Prepare the cream for the outside and pipe it on the surface with a flat pastry tip.
Smooth the mixture on the ends of the log and branches with a spatula.
Freeze until ready to serve, decorate with truffles, chocolate curls, meringue mushrooms and small holiday figures.

113

Baked Alaska «Saint Sylvestre»

A «Baked Alaska» can be made with any combination of flavors and can be served for any special occasion.
The marriage of fresh mint, strawberry and peach in this dessert is original and especially refreshing. Canned or freshly poached peaches can be used and raspberry sorbet can be substituted for strawberry.
It is served on a rectangular platter with a slice cut from the end.

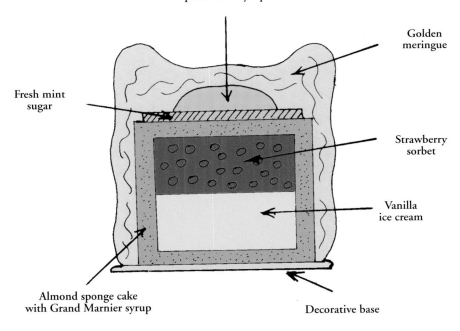

Peaches poached in syrup

Golden meringue

Fresh mint sugar

Strawberry sorbet

Vanilla ice cream

Almond sponge cake with Grand Marnier syrup

Decorative base

Golden meringue
400 g (14 oz/2 cups) sugar
150 ml (5 fl oz) water
8 egg whites
3 egg yolks
100 g (3 1/2 oz) sugar

Grand Marnier syrup
1/2 cup sugar syrup (1/4 cup each water, sugar)
1/4 cup Grand Marnier

Strawberry sorbet
1 kg (2 lbs) strawberry purée
500 ml (2 cups) water
450 g (15 oz) sugar
100 g (3 1/2 oz) trimoline
2.5 g (1/12 oz) stabilizer
Juice of 2 lemons

Procedure
Vanilla ice cream
Bring the milk and cream to a boil, add the split vanilla bean, cover and remove from heat.
Mix a little of the sugar with the stabilizer, set aside, and beat the remaining sugar with the egg yolks.
Bring the milk back to a simmer and stir in the dry milk powder.
Pour a little hot milk over the egg yolks, then transfer all the egg yolks into the hot milk and add the trimoline and stabilizer.
Return to medium low heat and cook the mixture to 85 C (185 F), the custard will coat a spoon.

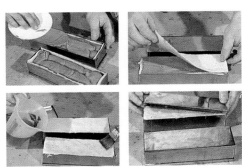

Ingredients
(for 4 desserts)

Almond sponge cake
2 cakes 40 X 60 cm (16 X 24 in)
450 g (15 oz) almond paste
6 eggs
60 g (2 oz) flour
8 egg whites
50 g (1 2/3 oz) sugar
30 g (1 oz) butter, melted

Vanilla ice cream
1 L (1 qt) milk
250 ml (1 cup) heavy cream
1 vanilla bean, split
250 g (8 oz) sugar
30 g (1 oz) non fat dry milk powder
180 g (6 oz) egg yolks
50 g (1 2/3 oz) trimoline
5 g (1/6 oz) stabilizer

Pour the custard through a sieve and cool quickly over ice.
Cover and refrigerate several hours before churning.

Almond sponge cake

Mix the eggs into the almond paste until smooth.
Beat the egg whites to soft peaks, add the sugar a little at a time and continue to beat to firm peaks.
Stir the flour into the almond paste mixture. Gently incorporate the beaten egg whites into the almond paste then fold in the melted butter. Spread the batter on two baking sheets lined with parchment paper and bake in a preheated 250 C (500 F) oven, 2-3 minutes or until set. As soon as the cakes are out of the oven, slide them off the baking sheets onto the work surface to cool quickly and stay moist.

Strawberry sorbet

Mix a little sugar with the stabilizer and set aside. Mix the strawberry purée, remaining sugar and water.
Blend in the trimoline then the stabilizer, whisking constantly so that no lumps are formed.
Stir in the lemon juice, pour the mixture through a sieve, cover and refrigerate several hours before churning.

Golden meringue

Cook the 400 g (2 cups) sugar and water to 118 C (245 F).
Beat the egg whites to soft peaks, with the mixer on low speed, pour the hot sugar syrup over the egg whites and continue to beat until cool.

Beat the 100 g (1 cup) sugar with the egg yolks until thick and lemon-colored. Fold the beaten egg yolks into the Italian meringue.
Note: To prepare a cooked egg yolk mixture, make a sugar syrup and proceed like the Italian meringue.
Use this golden meringue to cover the outside of the Baked Alaska.

Mint sugar

Use fresh mint leaves for this preparation. Be sure that the taste of the mint is not too strong.

Chop finely the washed leaves of one small bunch of mint.

Add about the same amount of sugar, mix and add a little green food color of desired. Store in the freezer in an air tight container.

Order of procedure and assembly

Cut the sponge cake to fit the sides of the mold, line the molds with cake and moisten with Grand Marnier syrup.

Pipe a layer of vanilla ice cream in the bottom, smooth the top then pipe strawberry sorbet to the top.

Place a layer of the sponge cake on top, moisten with syrup.

Cover each cake and place in the freezer several hours.

Drain the canned or freshly poached peaches (4-6 peach halves per cake.)

Prepare the fresh mint sugar.

Prepare the golden meringue: make the Italian meringue, beat the egg yolks and fold into the egg whites.

Spread the golden meringue over the desserts and apply some it in a decorative design with a piping bag and plain tip.

Sprinkle with powdered sugar and place in the freezer.

Preheat the oven to 220-250 C (450-500 F).

Place the desserts in the oven a few seconds, just long enough to brown the meringue.

Place in the freezer until ready to serve.

«La Troïka»

In France a «Baked Alaska» is called a «Norwegian omelette». This «omelette» has a Russian accent with a layer of orange-flavored vodka sorbet. It is combined with grape sorbet and wrapped in pistachio almond sponge cake.
The «runners» that transform this log shape into a «sled» are made separately of Swiss meringue and put into place just before the dessert is browned in the oven.
This original dessert would be a festive finale for a winter holiday meal.

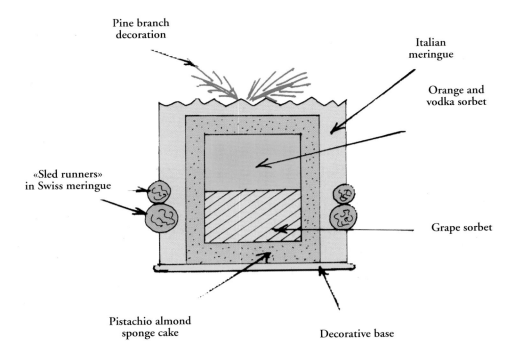

Pine branch decoration

Italian meringue

Orange and vodka sorbet

«Sled runners» in Swiss meringue

Grape sorbet

Pistachio almond sponge cake

Decorative base

Ingredients

Swiss meringue (for «sled runners»)
60 ml (2 fl oz) egg whites
125 g (4 oz) sugar
125 g (4 oz) powdered sugar

Italian meringue (for covering the desserts)
250 ml (1 cup) egg whites
500 g (8 oz) sugar
120 ml (4 fl oz) water

Pistachio almond sponge cake
450 g (15 2/3 oz) almond paste
5 eggs
60 g (2 oz) ground pistachios
80 ml (1/3 cup) milk
60 g (2 oz) flour
250 ml (4 fl oz) egg whites
80 g (2 2/3 oz) sugar

Muscat grape sorbet
(raspberry or peach sorbet (made from «wine» (red-tinted) peaches can be substituted)
1 L (1 qt) muscat grape juice
450 g (15 oz) sugar
50 g (1 2/3 oz) trimoline
600 ml (20 fl oz) water
5 g (1/6 oz) stabilizer

Juice of 1 lemon

Organage-flavored vodka sorbet
1 L (1 qt) fresh orange juice (about 15 oranges)
200 ml (7 fl oz) vodka
350 g (12 oz) sugar
70 g (2 1/3 oz) trimoline
5 g (1/6 oz) stabilizer

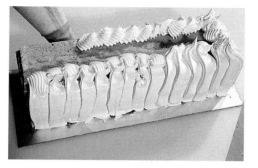

Procedure

Swiss meringue (for the «sled runners»)

Beat the egg whites to soft peaks, add the granulated sugar, beat on high speed until firm and glossy peaks are formed. Stir the powdered sugar in by hand.
With a piping bag fitted with a 8 mm (1/3 inch) plain tip, form the sled runners on a baking sheet lined with parchment paper (draw the forms in advance on the paper and trace with the meringue.)
Place in a warm oven overnight until hard.

Pistachio almond sponge cake

Beat the almond paste and eggs together until smooth and light.
Stir the milk into the ground pistachios, then mix into the almond paste mixture.
Beat the egg whites to firm peaks with the sugar.
Gently incorporate the beaten egg whites into the other mixture, sprinkling the flour over the top a little at a time as the batter is combined.
Spread the mixture on two baking sheets covered with parchment paper.
Bake in a preheated oven190-200 C (375-400 F) about five minutes or until set. Slide the cakes off the bakig sheets as soon as they come out of the oven to keep them drying out.

Grape sorbet

Mix the stabilizer with a little sugar and set aside.

Mix the remaining sugar, grape juice and water. Check the density (1147 D) and add water or sugar if necessary.

Whisk in the stabilizer and lemon juice.

Cover and refrigerate several hours before churning.

Transfer to the mold from the ice cream maker while the texture is still creamy.

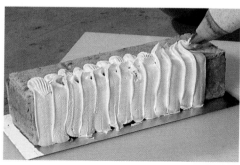

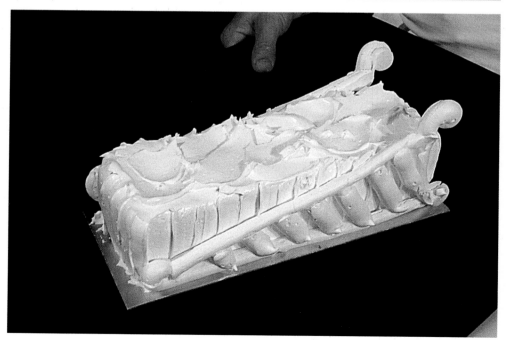

Fill the molds with the vodka sorbet and smooth the top. Place sponge cake on top.
Cover and place in the freezer several hours.

Unmolding and Decorating

Make the Italian meringue.
Unmold the cakes by warming the molds with a blowtorch or immersing them briefly in hot water.
Use a flat pastry tip to pipe an even layer of the meringue over the outside of the cake and smooth the top with a spatula.
Place the «runners», that were made in advance, on the sides to make the dessert look like a sled.
Place the dessert immediately into a preheated 250 C (500 F) oven for a few seconds to brown the meringue a little.
Take the dessert off the warm baking sheet and return to the freezer to keep the sorbets from melting. (The meringue cannot stay in the freezer too long.)
To serve, add a few holiday figures and sprinkle with powdered sugar.

Orange-flavored vodka sorbet

Mix the orange juice, trimoline, and sugar (mix a little with the stabilizer).
Verify the density (1147 D) and add water or sugar if necessary.
Whisk in the stabilizer and the vodka.
Churn the mixture and transfer to the mold immediately.
Note: If the sorbet is blended in advance, add the vodka just before churning. The alcohol may dissipate if it stands with the mixture too long and the flavor as well as the digestive qualities of the alcohol would be lost.

Italian meringue

Cook the water and sugar to the soft ball stage, 115 C (240 F)
Beat the egg whites to soft peaks, then, with the mixer on medium speed, pour the hot syrup into the egg whites. Continue to beat until the meringue is cooled.

Assembling the «Troika»

Cut each sheet cake in half and line the rectangular molds with cake. Set aside the remaining cake for the top.

Pipe the grape sorbet into each mold (using a piping bag with a large tip or no tip), fill each mold about halfway and smooth the top. Place in the freezer to firm.

Meanwhile, prepare the orange/vodka sorbet and churn.

"La Bûche Dorothée"

This log cake, rolled around the sorbet filling rather than molded, combines the delicate flavors and colors of pear, pistachio, almond and chocolate mousse with a hint of Kirsch.

This dessert could be served for tea or as an after dinner dessert. Each log cake or «bûche» serves 8-12. Individual portions can be accompanied by a pear coulis or a dollop of whipped cream.

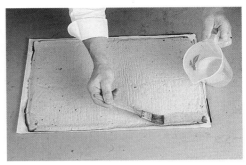

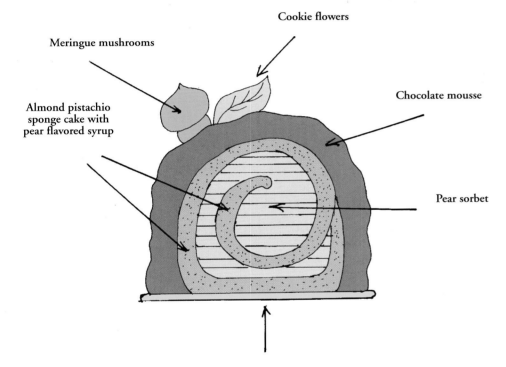

Meringue mushrooms

Cookie flowers

Almond pistachio sponge cake with pear flavored syrup

Chocolate mousse

Pear sorbet

Decorative base

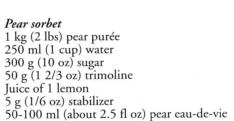

Pear sorbet
1 kg (2 lbs) pear purée
250 ml (1 cup) water
300 g (10 oz) sugar
50 g (1 2/3 oz) trimoline
Juice of 1 lemon
5 g (1/6 oz) stabilizer
50-100 ml (about 2.5 fl oz) pear eau-de-vie

Pear-flavored sugar syrup
1 cup sugar syrup
1/2 cup pear eau-de-vie

Meringue mushrooms
8 egg whites
250 g (8 oz) sugar
250 g (8 oz) powdered sugar, sifted

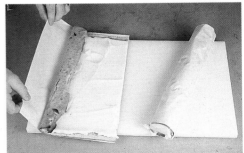

Ingredients

Chocolate mousse
Equal amounts:
Bombe mixture
Chocolate ganache (softened)
Whipped cream

Almond pistachio sponge cake
450 g (15 oz) almond paste
6 eggs
250 ml (1 cup/8) egg whites
80 g (2 2/3 oz) sugar
60 g (2 oz) pistachio paste
30 g (1 oz) melted butter

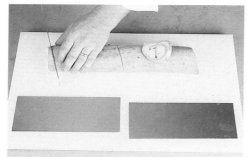

Procedure

Almond pistachio sponge cake

Melt the butter and set aside to cool to room temperature.

Beat the egg yolks with the almond paste until light and creamy.

Beat the egg whites to soft peaks then gradually add the sugar and continue beating to firm peaks.

Stir a little of the egg whites into the pistachio paste.

Gently fold the egg yolks/almond paste and pistachio paste (with a little green food color if desired) into the egg whites, then the cooled melted butter.

Spread the batter on 2 baking sheets (40 X 60 cm (16 X 24 in)) lined with parchment paper and bake at 220 C (425 F) 3-5 minutes without browning.

Slide the cakes off the hot baking sheets onto the work surface to cool quickly.

Pear sorbet

Mix a little sugar with the stabilizer, blend the remaining sugar with the fruit purée (very ripe or lightly poached fruit puréed with a little lemon juice) and water.

Stir in the trimoline, stabilizer and lemon juice.

Strain, cover and refrigerate several hours before churning.

Chocolate mousse

The ganache (see «Le Périgourdin») should be soft but not warm.

Stir an equal amount of cold bombe mixture into the cool ganache then fold in an equal amount of whipped cream.

This mixture is piped on the dessert.

Meringue mushrooms

Beat the egg whites to soft peaks then gradually add the sugar and continue to beat to firm peaks.

Sift the powdered sugar over the meringue and carefully fold in.

With a small plain pastry tip, pipe the stems of the «mushrooms» on baking sheets lined with parchment paper. With a slightly larger tip, pipe the «caps» on separate baking sheets and sprinkle with cocoa.

Bake at about 100 C (200 F) until crisp.

Use a little meringue to adhere the stems to the caps and bake again to set the meringue.

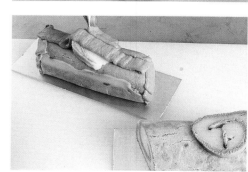

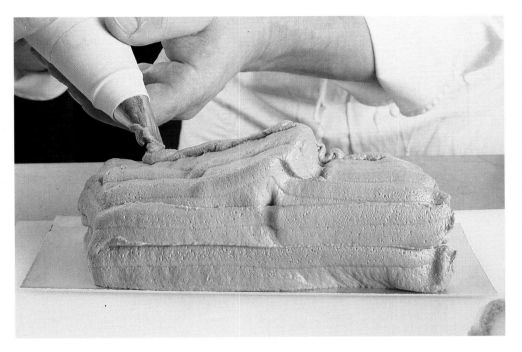

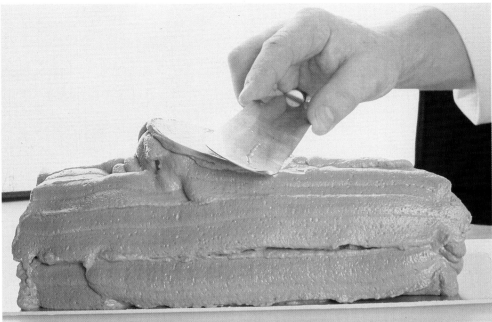

Order of preparation and assembly

Forming the roulade:

Moisten each sheet of sponge cake.

Churn the pear sorbet and while it is still creamy, spread the sorbet in an even layer over the cake.

Cut each cake in half, lengthwise. Use the edge of the parchment paper to roll each log from one end, removing the paper as it pushes the cake into a rolled shape.

Fill in the ends of each roulade with sorbet, using a spatula.

Cover and place immediately in the freezer.
Trim the ends and place the pieces of cake on top of each «log» to form the sawed off «branches.» Prepare the chocolate mousse with the ganache, bombe mixture and whipped creamn and cover each roulade using a piping bag or spatula.

Dip a spatula in hot water and smooth the ends of each cake.

Decorate with meringue mushrooms and cookie flowers.

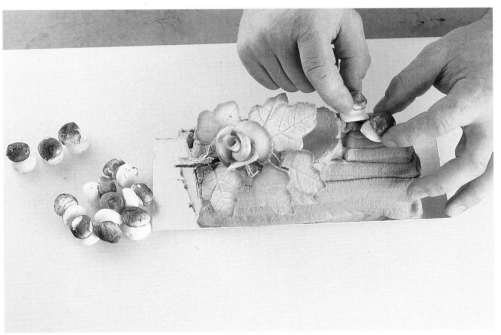

Frozen Nougat

One of the best traditional candies of France is the nougat of Montélimar in the Rhône valley. Like the candy, this frozen dessert is also made with honey, nuts and candied fruits and the shape, taste and texture is similar to the candy.

This dessert is ideal for any occasion, complimented by a sauce added to the plate just before serving. In summer, a coulis of red fruits is pretty and delicious while in winter a hot chocolate sauce would be perfect.

Another possibility is to cover a slice of the frozen nougat with sweetened apple purée and warm it briefly in the microwave which melts it slightly and brings out its flavor and perfume. The preparation is relatively easy: an Italian meringue combined with whipped cream and chopped fruits and nuts.

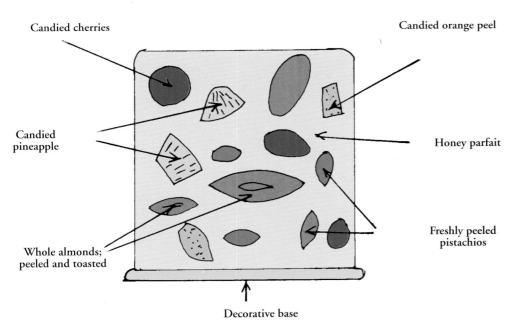

Candied cherries

Candied orange peel

Candied pineapple

Honey parfait

Whole almonds; peeled and toasted

Freshly peeled pistachios

Decorative base

Procedure

Place the pans (8 X 30 X 6 cm (3 1/4 X 12 X 2 1/4 in)) in the freezer.

Note that this dessert can be made in other molds, but the loaf pan most resembles the nougat confection. (Lining the molds with parchment will facilitate unmolding.)

Ingredients

(30 servings)

Nougat:
1 tsp vanilla extract
100 g (3 1/2 oz) sugar
220 g (7 2/3 oz) fragrant honey
250 L (1 cup) fresh egg whites
1 L (1 qt) heavy cream

Fruit and nut assortment:
120 g (scant 4 oz) candied orange peel
120 g (scant 4 oz) candied cherries
120 g (scant 4 oz) candied pineapple, cut in pieces
360 g (12 oz) toasted blanched almonds
80 g (2 2/3 oz) freshly peeled pistachios

127

Making the nougat:

Meringue:

In a copper sugar pot or stainless steel pan, simmer the sugar, honey and water to about 105 C (about 200 F.) At this moment, start beating the egg whites on high speed (to soft peaks.)
When the sugar reaches 123 C (255 F), pour it slowly into the egg whites with mixer on low speed. Continue to beat until the meringue is cool.

Cream:

Whip the cream to soft peaks in a chilled bowl (when too firm-ly whipped, it is more difficult to fold in.)

Assembly of honey parfait:

Fold the whipped cream into the cooled meringue along with the fruits and nuts and vanilla.

Transfer the mixture to the chilled molds, cover and return to the freezer.

To unmold, warm the molds with a blow torch or dip in a basin of hot water, invert onto a pan, wrap well with plastic wrap and freeze until ready to serve.

Advice for assembly

When folding the components together, add the fruits and nuts so that they are evenly dispersed throughout the mixture.

The mixture will be firm enough to hold the fruits and nuts in place without settling to the bottom.

Serving the frozen nougat

When ready to serve, unwrap the nougat and place on a cutting board. Cover loosely with plastic wrap and place in the refrigerator about 30 minutes to soften slightly.

Straight from the freezer, it will be too hard and brittle and may break and crack when sliced. The nougat should be firm and tender (but not melting) when sliced.

Arlette Goubier

Chapter 5 - Innovative Frozen Desserts

Sea Urchin   Champagne Cork   Beehive   Frozen Cherry Soufflé

"Le Mexicain"   Clown   Frozen Koughlof   Snowball

Sea Urchin

This original dessert is surprisingly easy to make. Since it is made with just one flavor of parfait, the molds are simply filled then placed in the freezer. The chocolate mousse coating is applied with a spatula which is pulled straight up to create the look of the sea urchin.

The Cognac parfait with candied chestnuts is a wonderful combination for a winter holiday meal. For a children's party, the Cognac parfait can be replaced with another flavor that goes well with chocolate.

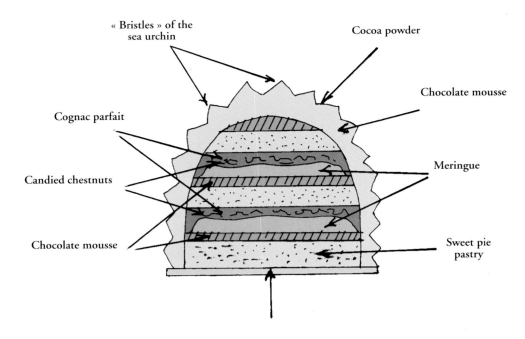

« Bristles » of the sea urchin

Cocoa powder

Chocolate mousse

Cognac parfait

Meringue

Candied chestnuts

Chocolate mousse

Sweet pie pastry

Decorative base

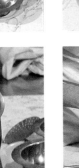

Ingredients

(For 8 desserts to serve 6 persons each)

Chocolate mousse
1 L (1 qt) heavy cream, whipped
600 g (1 lb 3 1/2 oz) bittersweet chocolate, chopped

Cognac parfait
16 egg yolks
400 g (14 oz) sugar syrup
1 L (1 qt) heavy cream
150 ml (scant 3/4 cup) Cognac
Candied chestnuts, chopped

133

Procedure

Cognac parfait

Make the bombe mixture:

Combine the egg yolks and syrup in the top of a double boiler. Whisk over high heat until the mixture thickens and warms to 80 C (175 F.)

Transfer to a mixer and beat until cool.

Beat the heavy cream in a chilled bowl to firm peaks.

Fold the cognac and whipped cream and chopped candied chestnuts into the bombe mixture.

Transfer the parfait immediately to the chilled molds.

Cover and place in the freezer several hours.
Warm the molds with a blow torch to remove them and return the desserts to the freezer.

Place each demi sphere of parfait on a circle of baked sweet pie pastry (optional.) The crisp pastry adds a nice crunch to the dessert.

Chocolate mousse

Melt the chocolate and cool.

Beat the cream to soft peaks in a chilled bowl. Fold the cream into the chocolate.

Just before serving, spread with the chocolate mousse over the round parfaits and pull straight up with the spatula at even intervals to form bristles.

The sea urchins can be served like this or for an even better effect, sprinkle with a little cocoa powder.

Champagne Cork

Wine sorbets have become a popular way to refresh one's palate between courses of a mulit-course dinner. Light and easy on the digestion, this dessert can be served during the meal as described or as the dessert course following a copious repast.
The forms can be made in individual portions which facilitates service for large groups.

Decoration
Almond paste
Melted chocolate in paper cone
Melted chocolate in spray gun

Decorations in chocolate
and almond paste

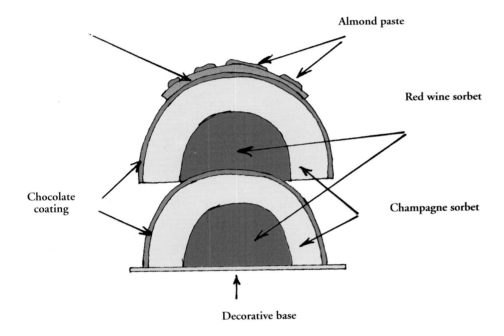

Almond paste

Red wine sorbet

Champagne sorbet

Chocolate coating

Decorative base

Ingredients

(80 portions or 10 liters (about 10 quarts) of sorbet (5 of each flavor.))

Champagne sorbet
1.8 L (7 1/3 cups) water
1.4 kg (1 lb 14 oz/7 cups) sugar
100 g (3 1/2 oz) trimoline
100 g (3 1/2 oz) powdered glucose
20 g (2/3 oz) stabilizer
Juice of 3 lemons
4 bottles good quality brut Champagne

Red wine sorbet
1.5 L (6 cups) water
1.2 kg (6 cups) sugar
200 g (7 oz) trimoline
20 g (2/3 oz) stabilizer
4 bottles good quality dry red wine
Candied chestnuts, chopped coarsely

Procedure

Champage sorbet

Place the molds in the freezer.

Mix 1 cup of sugar with the stabilizer, set aside.

Combine the remaining sugar, water, trimoline and glucose and simmer to make a syrup.

Whisk in the stabilizer and blend well.

When the syrup is cool, stir in the lemon juice and Champagne.

Churn right away then spread an even layer on the inside of the chilled molds, as shown.

Cover and place in the freezer.

Red wine sorbet

Mix 1 cup sugar with the stabilizer (if using), set aside.

Combine the remaining sugar, water, trimoline and glucose and simmer to make a syrup.

Whisk in the stabilizer and blend well.

When the syrup is cool, stir in the red wine.

Churn right away and fill the lined molds with the freshly churned sorbet.

Press the pieces of candied chestnuts into the red wine sorbet.

Place in the freezer several hours, unmold (warm the molds with a blow torch) then return to the freezer until ready to decorate.

Before serving, the desserts can be placed on a sweet pie pastry base. The crispy pastry provides a nice contrast in textures.

Order of preparation and assembly

Churn the Champagne sorbet and line the molds.

Place in the freezer to harden.

Churn the red wine sorbet and fill the molds; add the chestnuts.

Freeze several hours, unmold, then assemble the «corks.»

Coat the desserts with melted chocolate using the spray gun.

Roll, out and shape the almond paste as shown and place on the dessert.

Decorate with the melted chocolate in the paper cone.

Beehive («Le Rucher»)

This dessert will delight children and adults alike!

The beehive-shaped frozen confection combines the rich sweetness of honey and strawberry with the spicy taste of mint.

The refreshing strawberry sorbet encloses a rich honey parfait (French parfait is a «bombe» mixture with whipped cream), molded in a conical «bombe» mold.

The frozen layers are then covered with mint-flavored meringue, piped to look like an old-fashioned straw beehive. Honey is not often used as the principle sweetener and flavoring in French desserts. It is recommeneded to choose a full-flavored honey but not one with too strong a taste of flowers or pine.

It is altogether fitting to decorate this elegant dessert with a few sugar flowers and leaves which makes it fancy enough for a child's birthday party or any festive occasion.

As the finale to a meal, this combination of flavors would marry well with Champagne or a Gewurztraminer.

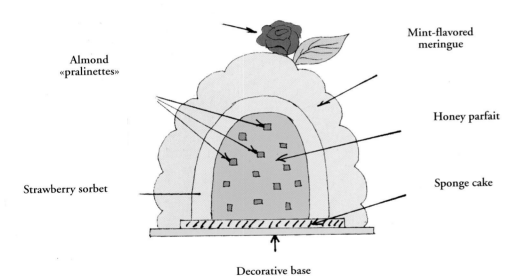

- Decoration
- Almond «pralinettes»
- Strawberry sorbet
- Decorative base
- Mint-flavored meringue
- Honey parfait
- Sponge cake

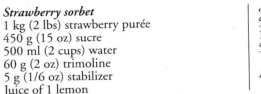

Strawberry sorbet
1 kg (2 lbs) strawberry purée
450 g (15 oz) sucre
500 ml (2 cups) water
60 g (2 oz) trimoline
5 g (1/6 oz) stabilizer
Juice of 1 lemon

«Pralinettes»
500 g (1 lb) sugar
150 ml (5 fl oz) water
500 g (1 lb) chopped almonds

Note: Each dessert requires a thin circle of sponge cake for the base.)

Ingredients
(for 4-5 desserts, serving 6-8 each)

Honey parfait
300 g (10 oz) honey
8 egg yolks
750 ml (3 cups) heavy cream
150 g (5 oz) pralinettes (see below)

Mint-flavored meringue
8 egg whites (250 ml/1 cup)
500 g (1 lb) sugar
100 ml (3.5 fl oz) water
2 g (1/12 oz) mint flavoring

Cover and refrigerate several hours before churning.

Honey parfait

Note that honey replaces the sugar syrup in this «bombe» mixture. Beat the egg yolks until thickened.

Meanwhile simmer the honey to 115 C (240 F). With the mixer at medium speed, pour the hot honey over the beaten yolks and continue to beat until cooled.

Beat the cream to firm peaks in a chilled bowl. Gently fold together the cooled egg yolk mixture, whipped cream and «pralinettes.»

Mint-flavored meringue

Cook the water and sugar to 115 C (240 F).

Meanwhile beat the egg whites to soft peaks. With the mixer on medium speed, pour the hot sugar syrup over the beaten egg whites and continue to beat until cooled.

Whisk in the mint flavoring and apply the meringue to the dessert immediately.

Almond «pralinettes»

Cook the water and sugar to 119 C (250 F). Add the chopped almonds.

Remove from the heat and stir to encourage the sugar to crystalize.

Return to the heat and cook until the mixture becomes golden brown.

Pour the mixture onto an oiled marble or baking sheet to cool. Break into small pieces and keep in an air tight container.

Procedure

Strawberry sorbet

Mix about 50 g (1/4 cup) sugar with the stabilizer and set aside.

Blend the remaining sugar and other ingredients together until the sugar has dissolved.

Verify the density (1147 D) then whisk in the stabilizer, stirring constantly to avoid lumps.

Decoration

Many decorations are suitable for a beehive shaped dessert-flowers with bees, small pots of honey or a piece of honeycomb.

For this dessert, the chef has modeled roses and leaves from almond paste.

Order of procedure and assembly

Place the «bombe» molds in the freezer.

Prepare the almond «pralinettes» and cool completely (these can be made several days in advance and kept in an air tight container.)

Prepare the strawberry sorbet.

Spread the freshly churned (soft, creamy texture) in an even 1.5 cm (1/2 inch) layer on the inside of the molds, place in the freezer for about 30 minutes.

Prepare the honey parfait with pralinettes.

Fill the molds with the parfait and smooth the tops.

Place a circle of sponge cake on the bottom, cover and place in the freezer about 2 hours.

Make the mint-flavored meringue.

While the meringue is cooling, unmold the «bombes» onto cardboard bases a little larger than the diameter of the molds.

Use a 12 mm (1/2 inch) plain tip to pipe the meringue around the frozen desserts to resemble beehives.

Sprinkle with powdered sugar.

Place the desserts on a double baking sheet and place into a preheated 250 C (500 F) oven a few seconds to brown the edges of the meringue and make the powdered sugar «pearl» a little.

Straight from the oven, transfer the «hives» to cold baking sheets and place them back in the freezer for about 1 hour.

Frozen Cherry Soufflé

This is an easy dessert to make and economical, too. The crispy pieces of meringue and cookies stirred into the soufflé mixture can be broken bits that cannot be used for another purpose.

Tart cherries are used here, but sweeter cherries can be substituted. It is recommended to use macerated fruits so that they remain soft when frozen. The macerated cherries can be replaced with another fruit, such as candied orange peel or raisins, according to availability.

The parfait mixture, flavored with cherry liqueur (or Grand Marnier or vanilla) is lightened with Italian meringue to give the airy mousse texture typical of cold soufflés. The dessert can be molded in any form you choose. A metal ring placed on a sheet pan lined with parchment paper is very practical. It can also be formed in a loaf pan to make square slices or in a large rectangular mold to cut portions of any size or shape. Serve slices of this frozen soufflé with an assortment of baked meringues and cookies.

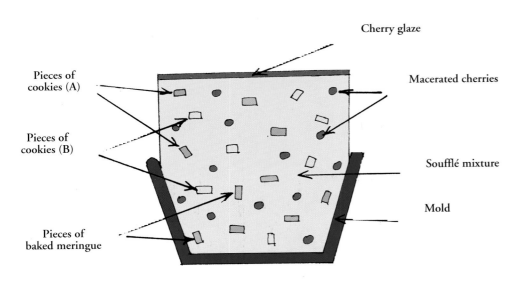

Cherry glaze

Pieces of cookies (A)

Macerated cherries

Pieces of cookies (B)

Soufflé mixture

Mold

Pieces of baked meringue

Ingredients

(For 25 servings)

Soufflé mixture
Bombe mixture:
8 egg yolks
260 g (8 1/3 oz) sugar
150 ml (5 fl oz) water

Whipped cream
800 ml (28 fl oz) heavy cream
250 ml (1 cup) cherry liqueur
    (or 200 ml (7 oz) Grand Marnier)
    or 1 tsp vanilla

Filling
150 g (5 oz) Swiss meringue, crumbled
200 g (7 oz) cookies, (two types, «A»,»B»)
1 kg (about 2 lbs) macerated cherries

Procedure

Frozen soufflés are not difficult to make. They are composed of three basic mixtures:

- bombe mixture
- whipped cream
- Italian meringue

Bombe mixture:

Make a sugar syrup with the water and sugar.

Combine with the egg yolks in a double boiler over very hot water and whisk until the mixture thickens. (Or pour hot syrup into egg yolks in mixer at medium speed.)

Beat at medium speed in a mixer until cool. The bombe mixture will be light and smooth. Refrigerate so that it does not deflate the whipped cream.

Adding the cream and meringue:

Make a an Italian meringue with 4 egg whites and beat until cool. Beat the cream in a chilled bowl and flavor with the liqueur.

Fold the cream and meringue into the cool bombe mixture.

146

Gently fold in the fruit and crumbled meringue and cookies and immediately transfer the mixture to the molds.

Dip a spatula in hot water to smooth the top so that the cherry glaze will be like a mirror (desserts like these are sometimes called «Miroir» in France.)

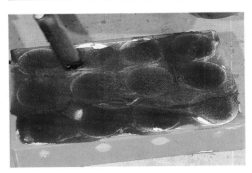

147

"Le Mexicain"

This refreshing parfait is molded in a conical mold and decorated with a nougatine sombrero and molded cookie poncho to resemble a Mexican enjoying a siesta under the hot sun.
The Tequila used to flavor the parfait follows the Mexican theme and adds a festive touch to this dessert.

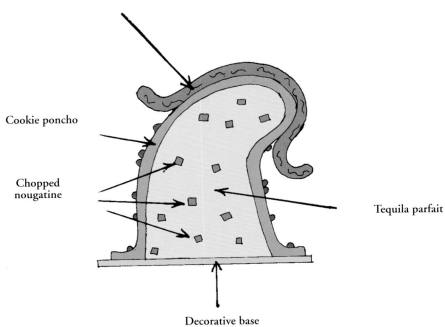

Nougatine sombrero

Cookie poncho

Chopped nougatine

Decorative base

Tequila parfait

Ingredients

(20 servings)

Tequila parfait
Bombe mixture:
16 egg yolks
400 g (14 oz) sugar syrup

1 L (1 qt) heavy cream
300 ml (10 fl oz) Tequila
(if not available, substitute rum, Kirsch, Cognac, Armagnac or Grand Marnier)

Nougatine (for hat)
600 g (3 cups) sugar
200 g (7 oz) sliced almonds

(Note that any strong alcohol can be used in this recipe.)

Gently fold the flavored cream into the cooled bombe mixture.

To further enhance the parfait, the trimmings from forming the nougatine sombrero can be chopped finely and folded into the parfait.

Procedure

Tequila parfait

Make the bombe mixture:

Combine the egg yolks and sugar syrup over very hot water in a water bath. Whisk as the mixture warms and thickens. Transfer to a mixer and beat on medium speed until cool.

Beat the cream to firm peaks in a chilled bowl. Stir in the Tequila.

149

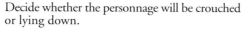

Decide whether the personnage will be crouched or lying down.

Nougatine sombrero

Lightly toast the sliced almonds.

In a heavy pot (preferably one made for melting sugar) slowly melt the sugar until it becomes golden brown.

Off the heat, stir in the toasted almonds.

When the nougatine has cooled enough to handle but is still warm enough to be pliable, form into the desired shapes.

Use oiled metal molds and cutters to shape the nougatine. Trimmings can be chopped and folded into the parfait.

As soon as the parfait is mixed, transfer it to the conical molds, as shown, cover and place in the freezer.

When the parfait has become firm, heat the mold with a blow torch and remove.

Return the unmolded parfait to the freezer until ready to assemble the dessert.

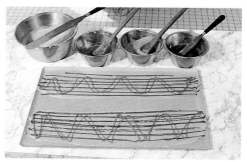

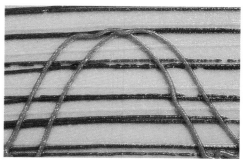

Molded cookie poncho

In France this cookie mixture is called «pâte à cornet» because it can be shaped while still warm from the oven to make «cornet» or cone shapes.

It is made with 1 kg (2 lbs) powdered almonds blended with 900 g (scant 2 lbs) sugar and moistened with enough egg whites to achieve a smooth batter.

This versatile mixture can be shaped into «tulips» to serve individual portions of ice cream or rolled around a spoon handle to make «cigarettes» or shaped into «cornets» or cones.

The possibilities are limited only by your imagination.

Using templates, this batter can be shaped into any sort of decoration. Food coloring can be used to tint some of the batter which can be piped in fanciful designs on plain batter for fantastic effects.

For this dessert, Mexican colors of red and brown were chosen to decorate the poncho which is given its final form while still warm from the oven.

Bake at 200 C (400 F) until very lightly browned. Watch them carefully during baking because they brown quickly.

Clown

Here is an amusing way to present a molded fozen dessert. It is especially appreciated by children. The same idea of making a head in ice cream can be used to make other characters as well.

The head is molded in an egg-shaped mold using layers of various ice creams and sorbets and so that each slice is pretty.

The same flavors used on the inside are used on the outside to decorate-raspberry sorbet for the nose and cocoa sorbet for the mouth. The hair is made with almond paste or a moldable chocolate mixture.

The molded ice base is not only decorative but also keeps the dessert from melting when served.

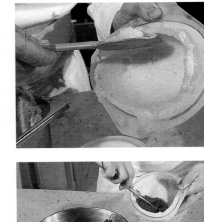

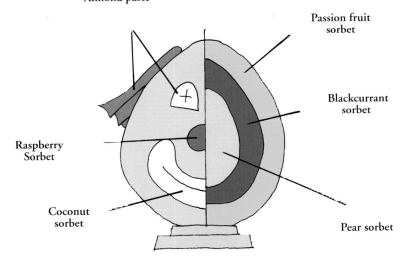

Almond paste

Passion fruit sorbet

Blackcurrant sorbet

Raspberry Sorbet

Coconut sorbet

Pear sorbet

Ice support

Assembly

The egg shaped mold for this dessert comes in two halves.

It is important that the molds are chilled in the freezer in advance so that the first layer of ice cream adheres to it.

Line the chilled molds with freshly churned ice cream, being very careful not to hold the mi\old in the warm palm of your hand which could melt the ice cream and spoil the appearance of the fininshed dessert.

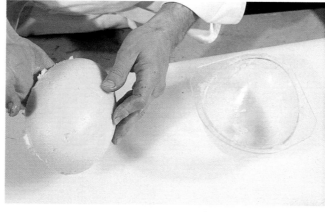

The first layer should be about 1.5-2 cm (1/2-3/4 in). As soon as the molds are lined, cover and place in the freezer for at least 1 hour.

Meanwhile, prepare the second flavor of ice cream of sorbet (choose a bright, contrasting color to make each slice pretty.

Apply the second layer, which will be thinner than the first (5-6 mm (1/4 inch), depending on the size of the mold. Return to the freezer to become firm.

Prepare the third flavor (in a contrasting color and flavor to the center layer), fill each half mold to the top, cover and place in the freezer for 1-2 hours.

Roll out small balls of white almond paste and paint a design with food color (here, the chef has used coffee syrup, a French ingredient.)

The hair

Color some almond paste with orange or brown food color (paste colors work best.)

Roll out a strip about 15 cm (5 in) wide and 30 cm (10 in) long and fold in half.

Cut through the folded end to form narrow strips (5 mm X 5 cm (1/4 in X 2 in) to make «locks» of hair.

Adhere the other ends of the almond paste togther with a little sugar syrup.

In a bowl, place 250 ml (1 cup) water.

Add 50 ml (scant 1/4 cup) of milk or 5 g (1 oz) milk powder (dissolved in a little water.)

Stir in a few drops of food color to make a pastel-colored base.

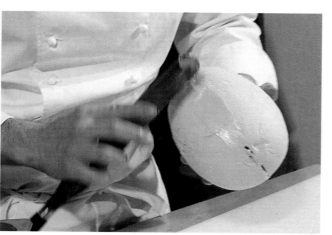

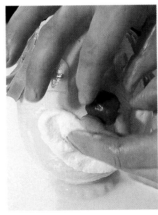

Pour the mixture into a ring mold or other shape that will suit the shape of the clown and be easily unmolded.
Place in the freezer several hours.
Place the mold in a large bowl of hot water, unmold and place in the freezer until ready to use.

Unmolding the clown

Fill a bowl, large enough to hold the mold, with warm water.
Place one half of the mold at a time into the water for a few seconds.
Pivot the loosened ice cream with one hand to create a little air pocket which will release the ice cream. Place it flat side down on a parchment lined sheet and place in the freezer.
Use some of the ice cream or sorbet from the outside layer to «glue» the two halves together.
Place the completed «head» on the unmolded pedestal.

Decorating the «Clown»

Soften a little ice cream of sorbet in a light color (left from filling the molds.)
Use a medium plain tip to pipe the mouth.
Scoop a small ball of raspberry sorbet (with a melon baller) for the nose.
Stick on the eyes and the hair with whipped cream.
Place the finished clown immediately into the freezer until ready to serve.

Frozen Koughlof

*Alsace, in eastern France is the inspiration for this pretty and refreshing deseert.
The fluted shape comes from the traditional «Kughlof» mold used in Alsace to make
a buttery yeast bread of the same name.
Two products of the region are used in the dessert-white wine sorbet (made with
Gewurztraminer) and a parfait flavored with «marc de Gewurtztraminer.»
This would be a special treat to serve at «tea time» in the afternoon and would be
especially appropriate to serve for dessert following a dinner of Alsatian dishes.*

Ingredients
(for about 80 servings)

Gewurztraminer sorbet
(makes about 6 L (6 qt))
150 g (5 oz) glucose
1 kg 450 g (3 lbs) sugar
20 g (2/3 oz) stabilizer
Juice of 4 lemons
4 bottles of Alsatian white wine

Parfait with Marc de Gewurztraminer
16 egg yolks
380 g (12 2/3 oz) sugar
600 ml (20 fl oz) heavy cream
150 ml (2/3 cup) marc de Gewurztraminer
300 g (10 g) white raisins macerated in
200 ml (7 fl oz) marc

Chocolate covering
200 g (7 oz) covering chocolate
200 g (7 oz) cocoa butter

Macerated raisins — White wine sorbet — Chocolate covering — Parfait with marc — Base

Procedure

Gewurztraminer sorbet
Blend 250 g (8 oz) sugar with the stabilizer and set aside.
Bring to a boil, 1.8 L (cups), 1.2 kg (2 1/2 lbs) sugar, and the glucose. As soon as the syrup comes to a boil, add the sugar/stabilizer mixture in a steady stream, whisking constantly. The syrup will thicken slightly and look like aspic. Cool the syrup and stir in the lemon juice and wine. Churn immediately.

Marc de Gewurztraminer parfait
To make the «bombe» mixture (similar to a sabayon), which is the base for all French «parfaits,» combine 16 egg yolks and a sugar syrup made with 280 ml (2 1/8 cups) water and 380 g (12 2/3 oz) sugar. Whisk over a water bath until mixture thickens like hollandaise. Continue to beat with a mixer until the mixture cools.
Meanwhile whip the cream to firm peaks and stir in the marc.
Fold the whipped cream and macerated raisins into the sabayon.

Chocolate covering
Melt the covering chocolate and the cocoa butter over a water bath and stir until smooth and warm the spray gun to 30-40 C (100 F)
Pour the mixture through a fine-meshed sieve and pour into the warmed reserve of the spray gun.

Assembly

Lining and filling the kughlof molds
In advance, place the molds in the freezer.
Make the sorbet and line the molds as soon as the sorbet is churned, when it is creamy and easy to spread.
Press against the sides of the mold with the spatula while applying the layer of sorbet to be sure there are no air bubbles.
Use the back of a spoon to even out the layer of sorbet and smooth the surface.
Scrape off any sorbet which is over the edge of the mold.
Cover and place in the freezer to become firm. Make the parfait mixture and as soon as it is churned, fill the molds to the top. Smooth the top, cover and place in the freezer.

Unmolding and decorating
When both layers have become completely frozen, proceed with unmolding and decorating:
*Place the mold in a bowl of warm water for a few seconds to loosen the sides from the mold.
*Unmold onto a decorative base.
*Place in the freezer to firm the outside.
*Meanwhile, prepare the chocolate mixture and place in the spray gun and prepare an area with a sheet or newspapers to catch the spray of chocolate.
*Place the frozen koughlof on the counter and spray evenly with chocolate. It is recommended to spray twice for a thick, dark coat of chocolate. Keep the koughlof frozen until ready to sell in a shop or serve in a restaurant or at home.

Snowball ("Boule de Neige")

Balls of crushed ice with fruit juice or honey were probably the first iced confections, a dessert enjoyed early in culinary history.
In modern French cooking there is a fudge-like cake called a «boule de neige» which is molded in a dome-shaped mold and piped with rosettes of whipped cream to resemble a snowball. This frozen dessert, also coated in whipped cream, can be made with a layer of chocolate ice cream on the outside like the cooked dessert, however the bright color of the passion fruit sorbet makes the slices prettier and more refreshing.
The combination of flavors can be determined by taste or availability:

- *Lemon sorbet with red fruit mousse*
- *Passion fruit sorbet with Kirsch parfait*
- *Pear sorbet with chocolate parfait on the inside*
- *Champagne sorbet with Marc parfait.*

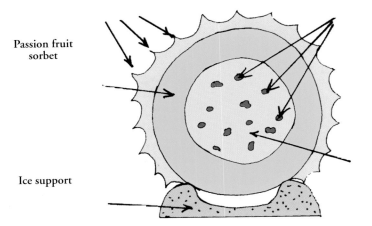

Whipped cream decoration

Macerated candied fruit

Passion fruit sorbet

Frozen kirsch mousse

Ice support

Ingredients

(36 servings)

Passion fruit sorbet
1 L (1 qt) passion fruit juice
600 g (3 cups) sugar
200 g (7 oz) trimoline
10 g (1/3 oz) stabilizer

Frozen Kirsch mousse
250 ml (1 cup) whole milk
8 egg yolks
200 g (1 cup) sugar
500 ml (2 cups) heavy cream
125 ml (1/2 cup) Kirsch

Whipped cream decoration
1 L (1 qt) heavy cream
150 g (5 oz) powdered sugar
Vanilla or Kirsch to flavor

Filling (optional)
Macerated candied fruits
Macerated poached fruits
Pieces of baked meringue
Pieces of cookies

Procedure

Passion fruit sorbet

Mix 100 g (1/2 cup) sugar with the stabilizer.

Combine the remaining sugar with the water and trimoline, bring to a simmer. Whisk the stabilizer into the simmering syrup.

Cool the syrup then stir in the passion fruit juice.

Strain and churn and spread an even layer in the molds while the sorbet is creamy.

Note: Passion fruit is a popular flavor in France, especially for frozen desserts. Frozen passion fruit juice is available to professional chefs. While the fresh fruit gives a more intense flavor than the pasteurized product, it is very expensive and time consuming to produce enough juice for a recipe like this.

Frozen Kirsch mousse

Make a custard (crème anglaise) with the milk, egg yolks and sugar.

Whisk the custard in the mixer until it cools completely.

Cover and place in the freezer to set.

Meanwhile beat the cream to firm peaks and flavor with Kirsch. Fold the whipped cream into the cooled custard (and the fruits/meringue/cookies if using) and fill the molds.

Order of preparation and assembly

Techniques for lining molds with sorbet:

Place the molds in the freezer several hours in advance.

Spread a thick layer of sorbet, pressing well to eliminate air bubbles.

Scoop out the center with a spoon to make an even layer and smooth the surface with the back of the spoon dipped in hot water.

Trim the edges, cover and freeze to harden.

Fill the center with freshly prepared mousse, smooth the top, cover and return to the freezer several hours.

Chap. 6 - Additional Recipes and Information

Tricks of the trade

Contents

How to keep frozen desserts from melting while assembling

Place ice cubes in a deep sided jelly roll or hotel pan and place another baking sheet on top. Keep the elements of the frozen dessert on this chilled surface while assembling and decorating.

How to augment flavor

*Add a little cocoa to intensify the flavor of coffee or chestnut desserts.
* Add a little coffee syrup (ingredient used for flavor and color in French pastry making) to chocolate ice cream.
*For caramel ice cream, cook the sugar in the recipe without water to the caramel stage. Add the cream in the recipe directly to the caramel to dissolve it and infuse a vanilla bean as well into the cream.
*Pepper can heighten certain flavors; a little finely ground white pepper can be used in chocolate and pistachio ice cream or wine and exotic fruit sorbets.

Trick for even layers

Prepare the filling for a layered frozen dessert and freeze it in a small mold. Unmold and keep frozen.

Prepare the sorbet or ice cream for the outside layer and line a larger mold with a thick layer of the mixture.

Press the smaller, premolded mixture into the center of the larger one and press until it is even with the rim. Scrape off excess mixture from the outer layer.

Place in the freezer several hours and unmold when firm.

Selecting flavors and colors that go together

In addition to choosing flavors that taste good together, there are two factors that determine the choice of mixtures:

A. Color

Dark colors overpower the presentation.
Use flavorful mixtures in deep hues on the inside or at the bottom of the frozen desserts. Use the lightest colors on the outside.

For example:

Lemon	Pineapple
Raspberry	Mango
Chocolate	Black currant
Vanilla	Strawberry
Praline	Raspberry
Chocolate	Black currant

B. Texture

To facilitate slicing, the firmest mixtures are placed in the center or at the bottom of frozen desserts. Mixtures that are very sweet and melt easily should be placed on the outside or at the top.

For example:

Raspberry	Lemon
Vanilla	Black currant
	Chocolate
Strawberry	Champagne
Praline	Raspberry
	Vanilla

Which flavors go well together?

Flavor combinations are a matter of personal taste. Almost any combination can be good if the ice cream or sorbet is well made with the right level of flavoring.
*Strong flavorings and fruits with a high acid content should be used carefully so that the mixtures made with them are not too overpowering.
*Acidity, in a well made fruit sorbet can accentuate the taste of a mixture with a more subtle flavor.
*Avoid combining two mixtures with high acidity in the same dessert.
*With the exception of the «Rainbow» dessert, it is recommended to combine no more than three flavors in one dessert as it is very difficult to distinguish the different tastes.

What beverages are good with frozen dessets?

Red fruit sorbets go well with sweet white wines like Sauternes, while fruits like peaches and melon are complimented by sweet red wines like Port.
Champagne and other bubbling wines go very well with ice cream and other cream-based frozen desserts.
Following an ice cream sundae, cold water is very refreshing and allows you to enjoy the taste sensation you've just had.

How to add fruit to ice cream and sorbets?

If diced fruit is added to a sorbet or ice cream, the water in the fresh fruit will harden in the frozen dessert and be unpleasnat to eat.
Macerate all fruit in a flavorful alcohol of some kind to lower the freezing temperature so they stay soft.

Principle categories of frozen desserts in France

Strict government regulations

The making of frozen desserts, or «glacerie» in France, is closely regulated by the government. There are specific formulas used by trained «glaciers» that have specific names: ice cream with eggs («glaces aux œufs»), frozen creams («crèmes glacées»), sorbets, parfaits, souffles, granités.
Some are more closely regulated than others, with required minimum amounts of certain ingredients. Artisan as well as professional producers follow these guidelines.
The basic formulas, determined by official French legislation, for several mixtures are outlined here. (US equivalents not given, for reference only.)

1. «Glace au sirop»

(Ice creams made wiht sugar syrup with fruits or natural favorings)

Minimum quantities for 100 g (3 1/2 oz) of product

A. Ice cream with syrup and fruits

25 g sugar
15 g sweet fruit
10 g tart fruit
30 g total in dry ingredients

Milk or cream can be added without changing the name of the product.

B. Ice cream with syrup and favorings

18 g sugar
2 g chocolate
3 g praline
2.5 g coffee
.1 g vanilla
3 g pistachiop
8 g caramel
28 g total in dry ingredients

162

2. «Glace aux œufs» (egg-based creams)

Milk or cream can be added without changing the name of the product.

Stabilizer (optional) is authorized at 1% for both categories.

Minimum quantities for 100 g (3 1/2 oz) of product

16 g sugar
6 g powdered glucose
Trimoline, as needed
7 g egg yolks
2 g butterfat

Natural flavorings

2 g chocolate
3 g praline
2.5 g coffee
.1 g vanilla
3 g pistachio
8 g caramel
29 g total in dry ingredients
1 g stabilizer

3. «Crèmes glacées»

Minimum quantities for 100 g (3 1/2 oz) product

A. «Crèmes glacées» with flavorings

14 g sugar
7 g butterfat
2 g chocolate
3 g praline
2.5 g coffee
.1 vanilla
3 g pistachio
8 g caramel
31 g total indry ingredients

B. «Crèmes glacées with fruits

14 g sugar
5 g butterfat
15 g sweet fruits
10 g tart fruits
29 g total in dry ingredients
1 g stabilizer

4. Fruit sorbets

Minimum quantities for 100 g (3 1/2 oz) of product

A. Sorbets made with sweet fruits

18 g sugar (saccarose)
6 g powdered glucose
Trimoline, as needed
35 g fruit purée
Pure water as needed
1 g stabilizer, maximum

B. Sorbets made with tart fruits

18 g sugar
6 g powdered glucose
Trimoline as needed
15 g tart fruits
Pure water as needed
1 g stabilizer, maximum

5. Sorbets made with wine and liqueurs

Minimum quantities for 100 g (3 1/2 oz) product

28 g sugar (saccarose)
6 g powdered glucose
Trimoline, as needed
Pure water as needed
Wine, liqueur as needed

Fruits sorbets

Apricot sorbet

Ingredients

500 g (1 b) apricots
180 g (6 oz) sugar
250 ml (1 cup) water
25 g (scant 1 oz) glucose
5 g (1/6 oz) stabilizer
Juice of 1 lemon
1 lemon

Procedure

Mix the stabilizer with 30 g (1 oz) sugar and set aside.
Combine the remaining sugar with the water and glucose, bring to a simmer and cool.
Place the apricots (cut in half/pit removed) and the lemon (cut in quarters) in the syrup and simmer until tender.
Purée the poached apricots and lemon in a food processor then whisk in the stabilizer.
Cool, check the densitity then cover and chill several hours to allow the flavor to delevop.
Churn in an ice cream machine.

Pineapple sorbet

Ingredients

500 g (1 lb) fresh pineapple purée
170 g (5 2/3 oz) sugar
250 ml (1 cup) water
10 g (1/3 oz) trimoline or honey
Juice of 1 lemon

Procedure

Stir all the ingredients together.
Cover and chill several hours to allow the flavor to develop.
Churn in an ice cream machine.

Note: A little rum can be added when the mixture is churned or add pieces of pineapple macerated in rum at the end of churning.

Variation

Pineapple sorbet

Ingredients

1 L (1 qt) pineapple pulp
250 ml (1 cup) water
300 g (10 oz) sugar
50 g (1 2/3 oz) trimoline
5 g (1/6 oz) stabilizer (optional)
Juice of 1 lemon

Banana sorbet

Ingredients

500 g (1 lb) peeled bananas
(2 lbs with peels)
180 g (6 oz) sugar
250 ml (1 cup) water
10 g (1/3 oz) trimoline or honey
Juice of 1 lemon

Procedure

Bring the water and sugar to a simmer to make a syrup, cool.
Stir in the lemon juice.
Peel the bananas, cut in large chunks and immerse in the cooled syrup to keep them from browning.
Purée the bananas with the syrup in a food processor and press through a sieve.
Cover and chill several hours then churn.

Variation

Banana sorbet

Ingredients

1 kg (2 lbs) banana purée
800 ml (3 1/3 cups) water
450 g (2 1/4 cups) sugar
50 g (1 2/3 oz) trimoline
5 g (1/6 oz) stabilizer
Juice of 2 lemons

Black currant sorbet

Ingredients

500 g (1 lb) black currant purée
180 g (6 oz) sugar
300 ml (10 fl oz) water
10 g (1/3 oz) trimoline
Juice of 1 lemon

Procedure

Blend all the ingredients.
Cover and chill several hours to allow the flavor to develop.
Check the density (1147 D) , add sugar or water as needed and churn.

Variation

Black currant sorbet

Ingredients

1 L (1 qt) fruit pulp
800 ml (3 1/3 cups) water
550 g 1 lb 1 2/3 oz) sugar
100 g (3 1/2 oz) trimoline
10 g (1/3 oz) stabilizer (optional)
Juice of 2 lemons

Cherry sorbet

Ingredients

500 g (1 lb) cherries
180 g (6 oz) sugar
250 ml (1 cup) water
50 g (1 2/3 oz) glucose
5 g (1/6 oz) stabilizer
Juice of 1 lemon

Procedure

Mix the stabilizer with 30 g (1 oz) sugar, set aside.
Make a syrup with the remaining sugar, water and glucose.
Poach the cherries in the syrup.
Press the cooked cherries through a sieve to eliminate the pits.
Whisk the stabilizer into the syrup and cherry purée.
Chill then add the lemon juice.
Check the density (1147 D), cover and chill several hours before churning.

Chestnut sorbet

Ingredients

400 g (14 oz) chestnut purée
180 g (6 oz) sugar
250 ml (1 cup) water
30 g (1 oz) honey)
10 ml (1/3 fl oz) Cognac
1 g (1/4 tsp) cocoa powder

Procedure

Bring the water to a simmer with the sugar.
Add the chestnut purée, honey and cocoa.
Cool then stir in the Cognac.
Check the density, cover and chill several hours before churning.

Note: Pieces of candied chestnuts can be added at the end of churning.

Fruits sorbets (continuation)

Lemon sorbet

Ingredients

250 ml (1 cup) fresh lemon juice
400 g (14 oz) sugar
500 ml (2 cups) water
100 g (3 1/2 oz) glucose
5 g (1/6 oz) stabilizer

Procedure

Mix 50 g (1/4 cup) sugar with the stabilizer, set aside.
Bring the water to a simmer with the remaining sugar, whisk in the stabilizer and cool.
Stir in the lemon juice and check the density.
Cover and chill several hours before churning.

Lime sorbet

Ingredients

250 ml (1 cup) fresh lime juice
400 g (14 oz) sugar
500 ml (2 cups) water
100 g (3 1/2 oz) glucose
5 g (1/6 oz) stabilizer

Procedure

Mix 50 g (1/4 cup) of the sugar with the stabilizer, set aside.
Bring the water to a simmer with the remaining sugar, whisk in the stabilizer and cool.
Stir in the lime juice and check the density.
Cover and chill several hours before churning.

Note: Candied lime peel, chopped finely, can be added at the end of churning.

Quince sorbet

Ingredients

600 g (1 lb 3 1/2 oz) quince
180 g (6 oz) sugar
500 ml (2 cups) water
20 g (2/3 oz) trimoline or honey
Juice of 1 lemon

Procedure

Peel the quince and remove the seeds and cut into large chunks.
Place the peels and water in a pot and place the fruit in a steamer basket above. Cook until the fruit is soft.
Strain the water and reserve 1 cup.
Purée the quince and press through a sieve.
Mix the quince purée, water, sugar, honey and lemon juice.
Check the density, cover and chill several hours before churning.

Strawberry sorbet

Ingredients

500 g (1 lb) strawberry purée
180 g (6 oz) sugar
250 ml (1 cup) water
25 g (scant 1 oz) trimoline
5 g (1/6 oz) stabilizer
Juice of 2 lemons

Procedure

Mix all the ingredients.
Cover and chill several hours to allow the flavor to develop.
Check the density and churn in an ice cream maker.

Raspberry sorbet

Ingredients

500 g (1 lb) seedless raspberry purée
180 g (6 oz) sugar
250 ml (1 cup) water
25 g (scant 1 oz) trimoline
5 g (1/6 oz) stabilizer
Juice of 2 lemons

Procedure

Mix all the ingredients.
Cover and chill several hours to allow the flavor to develop.
Check the density and churn in an ice cream maker.

Variation

Raspberry sorbet

Ingredients

1 kg (2 lbs) seedless raspberry purée
500 ml (2 cups) water
450 g (2 1/4 cups) sugar
100 g (3 1/2 oz) trimoline
5 g (1/6 oz) stabilizer (optional)
Juice of 1 lemon

Guava sorbet

Ingredients

500 g (1 lb) guava purée
180 g (6 oz) sugar
250 ml (1 cup) water
25 g (scant 1 oz) trimoline
5 g (1/6 oz) stabilizer
Juice of 2 lemons

Procedure

Mix all the ingredients.
Cover and chill several hours to allow the flavor to develop.
Check the density and churn in an ice cream maker.

Grenadine sorbet

Ingredients

500 g (1 lb) grenadine juice
200 g (7 oz/1 cup) sugar
250 ml (1 cup) water
25 g (scant 1 oz) trimoline
2 g (1/12 oz) stabilizer
Juice of 2 lemons

Procedure

Mix 50 g (1/4 cup) of the sugar with the stabilizer, set aside.
Bring the water, remaining sugar and trimoline to a simmer to make a syrup.
Whisk in the stabilizer and grenadine juice and bring to a simmer then cool quickly over ice.
Stir in the lemon juice, check the density then churn.

Fruits sorbets (continuation)

Morello cherry sorbet

Ingredients

500 g (1 lb) Morello cherries
180 g (6oz) sugar
250 ml (1 cup) water
50 g (1 2/3 oz) trimoline
5 g (1/6 oz) stabilizer
Juice of 1 lemon

Procedure

Mix 50 g (1/4 cup) sugar with the stabilizer, set aside.
Bring the water, remaining sugar and trimoline to a simmer to make a syrup.
Poach the cherries in the syrup then press through a sieve to eliminate the pits.
Whisk the stabilizer into the fruit purée with the syrup mixture.
Cool then stir in the lemon juice.
Check the density, cover and chill several hours to allow the flavor to develop then churn in an cream maker.

Note: A few drops of Kirsch can be added just before churning.

Red currant sorbet

Ingredients

500 g (1 lb) red currant purée
180 g (6 oz) sugar
250 ml (1 cup) water
25 g (scant 1 oz) trimoline
5 g (1/6 oz) stabilizer
Juice of 2 lemons

Procedure

Mix the stabilizer with 50 g (1/4 cup) sugar, set aside.
Bring the water, remaining sugar and trimoline to a simmer to make a syrup.
Whisk in the stabilizer and bring to a simmer.
Cool the mixture then stir in the lemon juice.
Check the density, cover and chill several hours to allow the flavor to develop before churning.

Variation

Red currant sorbet

Ingredients

1 L (1 qt) fruit pulp
800 ml (3 1/3 cups) water
500 g (1 lb) sugar
100 g (3 1/2 oz) trimoline
10 g (1/3 oz) stabilizer (optional)

Mandarine sorbet

Ingredients

500 ml (2 cups) mandarine juice
180 g (6 oz) sugar
200 ml (7 fl oz) water
10 g (1/3 oz) trimoline
5 g (1/6 oz) stabilizer
Juice of 1 lemon

Procedure

Mix all the ingredients, cover and chill several hours to allow the flavor to develop.
Check the density and churn in an ice cream maker.

Mango sorbet

Ingredients

500 g (1 lb) mango purée
180 g (6 oz) sugar
250 ml (1 cup) water
10 g (1/3 oz) trimoline
5 g (1/6 oz) stabilizer
Juice of 2 lemons

Procedure

Mix all the ingredients, cover and chill several hours to allow the flavor to develop.
Check the density and churn in an ice cream maker.

Variation

Mango sorbet

Ingredients

1 kg (2 lbs) mango purée
500 ml (2 cups) water
275 g (9 1/2 oz) sugar
5 g (1/6 oz) stabilizer (optional)
Juice of 2 lemons

Cantaloupe sorbet

Ingredients

500 g (1 lb) cantaloupe purée
120 g (scant 4 oz) sugar
10 g (1/3 oz) trimoline
5 g (1/6 oz) stabilizer
Juice of 1 lemon

Procedure

Choose very ripe cantaloupes. Remove the skin and seeds. Weigh 1 pound of fruit and purée in a food processor.
Mix the purée with the remaining ingredients, cover and chill several hours to allow the flavor to develop.
Check the density then churn in an ice cream maker.

Black raspberry sorbet

Ingredients

500 g (1 lb) seedless black raspberry purée
180 g (6 oz) sugar
200 ml (7 fl oz) water
10 g (1/3 oz) trimoline
5 g (1/6 oz) stabilizer
Juice of 1 lemon

Procedure

Mix all the ingredients, cover and chill several hours to allow the flavor to develop.
Check the density then churn in an ice cream maker.

Blueberry sorbet

Ingredients

500 g (1 lb) blueberry purée
180 g (6 oz) sugar
200 ml (7 fl oz) water
10 g (1/3 oz) trimoline
5 g (1/6 oz) stabilizer
Juice of 1 lemon

Procedure

Mix all the ingredients, cover and chill several hours to allow the flavor to develop.
Check the density then churn in an ice cream maker.

Fruits sorbets (continuation)

Coconut sorbet

Ingredients

500 g (1 lb) unsweetened coconut milk
180 g (6 oz) sugar
250 ml (1 cup) water
10 g (1/3 oz) trimoline
5 g (1/6 oz) stabilizer

Procedure

Mix the ingredients in a non reactive saucepan. Heat the mixture to 65 C (150 F). Cool to room temperature then cover and chill several hours to develop the flavor.
Check the density, adding sugar or water to achieve 1147 D.
Churn in an ice cream maker.

Coconut sorbet

Ingredients

1 L (1 qt) milk
1 L (1 qt) coconut pulp
130 g (4 oz) powdered milk
300 ml (10 fl oz) heavy cream
470 g (scant 1 lb) sugar
100 g (3 1/2 oz) dextrose
15 g (1/2 oz) stabilizer (optinal)

Orange sorbet

Ingredients

500 ml (2 cups) fresh orange juice
180 g (6 oz) sugar
100 ml (3.5 fl oz) water
10 g (1/3 oz) trimoline
5 g (1/6 oz) stabilizer
Juice of 2 lemons

Procedure

Bring the water to a simmer with the sugar and stabilizer to make a syrup.
Cool then stir in the orange juice, trimoline and lemon juice.

Cover and chill several hours to allow the flavor to develop.
Verify the density then churn in an ice cream maker.

Variation

Orange sorbet

Ingredients

1 L (1 qt) orange juice
160 ml (5.3 oz) water
380 g (12 2/3 oz) sugar
50 g (1 2/3 oz) trimoline
5 g (1/6 oz) stabilizer (optional)
Juice of 1 lemon

Grapefruit sorbet

Ingredients

500 ml (2 cups) fresh grapefruit juice
180 g (6 oz) sugar
100 ml (3.5 fl oz) water
10 g (1/3 oz) trimoline
5 g (1/6 oz) stabilizer
Juice of 2 lemons

Procedure

Bring the water to a simmer with the sugar and stabilizer to make a syrup.
Cool then stir in the grapefruit juice, trimoline and lemon juice.
Cover and chill several hours to allow the flavor to develop.
Check the density then churn in an ice cream maker.

Papaya sorbet

Ingredients

500 g (1 lb) papaya purée
180 g (6 oz) sugar
200 ml (7 fl oz) water
10 g (1/3 oz) trimoline
Juice of 2 lemons

Procedure

Bring the water to a simmer with the sugar and stabilizer to make a syrup.
Cool then add the papaya purée, trimoline and lemon juice.

Cover and chill several hours.
Check the density, adding water or sugar to achieve 1147 D.
Churn in an ice cream maker.

Passion fruit sorbet

Ingredients

500 g (1 lb) passion fruit juice
180 g (6 oz) sugar
300 ml (10 fl oz) water
10 g (1/3 oz) trimoline

Procedure

Mix all the ingredients.
Cover and chill several hours to develop the flavor.
Check the density then churn in an ice cream maker.

Variation

Passion fruit sorbet

Ingredients

1 L (1 qt) passion fruit juice
1 L (1 qt) water
600 g (3 cups) sugar
100 g (3 1/2 oz) trimoline
10 g (1/3 oz) stabilizer (optional)

Peach sorbet

Ingredients

500 g (1 lb) peaches
180 g (6 oz) sugar
250 ml (1 cup) water
25 g (scant 1 oz) trimoline
5 g (1/6 oz) stabilizer
Juice of 1 lemon
1 lemon

Procedure

Mix 30 g (1 oz) sugar with the stabilizer, set aside.
Bring the water, sugar and trimoline to a simmer to make a syrup.
Poach the peaches and the lemon (quartered) in the syrup. Remove the peach pits and purée the peaches and lemon in a food processor and press through a sieve.

Whisk the stabilizer into the mixture, cool then add the lemon juice.
Verify the density, cover and refrigerate several hours then churn in an ice cream maker.

Variation

Peach sorbet

Ingredients

1 kg peach puree
160 ml (5.3 fl oz) water
300 g (1 1/2 cups) sugar
100 g (3 1/2 oz) trimoline
5 g (1/6 oz) stabilizer (optional)
Juice of 1 lemon

«Wine» peach sorbet

(Sometimes called «blood» peaches, this fruit has deep red flesh.)

Ingredients

500 g (1 lb) red-fleshed peaches
180 g (6oz) sugar
125 ml (1/2 cup water
125 ml (1/2 cup) dry red wine
25 g (scant 1 oz) honey
5 g (1/6 oz) stabilizer
Juice of 1 lemon
1 lemon

Procedure

Mix 30 g (1 oz) sugar with the stabilizer, set aside.
Bring the water to a simmer with the remaining sugar, honey, and red wine.
Cut the peaches in half (keep the pit for flavor) and cut the lemon in quarters. Poach the fruit in the sugar syrup.
Purée the fruit in a food processor then whisk in the stabilizer.
Chill the mixture, check the density and churn.

Pear sorbet

Ingredients

500 g (1 lb) pears
180 g (6 oz) sugar
250 ml (1 cup) water
25 g (scnat 1 oz) trimoline
5 g (1/6 oz) stabilizer
Juice of 1 lemon

Procedure

Mix the stabilizer with 230 g (1oz) of the sugar, set aside.
Make a syrup with the water, remaining sugar and trimoline.
Peel and core the pears and cut them into quarters, poach in the syrup.
Purée the poached pears in a food processor, stir in the syrup then whisk in the stabilizer.
Cool then stir in the lemon juice, check the density.
Cover and chill several hours to develop the flavor then churn.

Note: Pear eau de vie can be added at the beginning of the churning process to intensify the fruit flavor.

Variation

Pear sorbet

Ingredients

1 kg (2 lbs) pear pulp
250 ml (1 cup) water
300 g (1 1/2 cups) sugar
100 g (3 1/2 oz) trimoline
5 g (1/6 oz) stabilizer (optional)
Juice of 1 lemon

Apple sorbet

Ingredients

500 g (1 lb) Granny Smith apples
180 g (6 oz) sugar
500 ml (2 cups) water
10 g (1/3 oz) honey or trimoline
Juice of 2 lemons

Procedure

Peel and core the apples and quarter the apples.
Place the peels, cores and water in the bottom of a non reactive pot and place the apples in a steamer basket above.
When the apples are soft, purée in a food processor. Strain the water and measure 250 ml (1 cup).
Mix the apple purée with the water, sugar, honey and lemon juice.
Check the density, cover and chill several hours before churning in an ice cream maker.

Note: To intensify the flavor of the apples, add a little Calvados or cider when the mixture is churned.

Variation

Apple sorbet

Ingredients

1 kg (2 lbs) apple pulp
300 ml (10 fl oz) water
300 g (10 oz/1 1/2 cups) sugar
75 g (2 1/2 oz) trimoline
5 g (1/6 oz) stabilizer (optional)
50 ml (1/4 cup) Calvados

Pumpkin sorbet

Ingredients

600 g (1 lb 3 1/2 oz) peeled fresh pumpkin
180 g (6 oz) sugar
500 ml (2 cups) water
20 g (2/3 oz) honey or trimoline
Juice of 1 lemon

Procedure

Steam the pumpkin and purée in a food processor.
Press the purée through a sieve and stir in 250 ml (1 cup) of the cooking water, the honey, sugar and lemon juice.
Check the density then cover and chill several hours before churning.

Note: For extra flavor, a little powdered cinnamon or ginger can be added when the mixture is churned.

Rhubarb sorbet

Ingredients

600 g (1 lb 3 1/2 oz) peeled rhubarb
180 g (6 oz) sugar
200 ml (7 fl oz) water
20 g (2/3 oz) glucose
Juice of 1 lemon
1/2 lemon
1/2 orange

Procedure

Cut the peeled rhubarb into chunks and cook slowly until soft with the sugar and citrus fruits (cut in pieces).
Remove the lemon and orange pieces, discard, then purée the cooked rhubarb in a food processor.
Add the water and lemon juice.
Check the density, cover and chill several hours to allow the flavor to develop before churning.

Tomato sorbet

Ingredients

500 g (1 lb) tomatoes
180 g (6 oz) sugar
200 ml (7 fl oz) water
25 g (scant 1 oz) glucose
5 g (1/6 oz) stabilizer

Procedure

Peel and seed the tomatoes.
Mix 30 g (1 oz) of the sugar with the stabilizer, set aside.
Bring the water to a simmer wiht the remaining sugar and glucose. Poach the tomatoes in the syrup then purée in the food processor.
Whisk in the stabilizer then cool the miixture.
Check the density the chill several hours before churning.

Note: For a more complex flavor, add white pepper or Tabasco, ketchup or celery seed.

Sorbets made with wines and liqueurs

Champagne sorbet

400 g (14 oz/2 cups) sugar
400 ml (14 fl oz) water
75 cl (1 bottle/3 cups) dry Champagne
5 g (1/6 oz) stabilizer
Grated zest of 1/2 lemon

Procedure

Mix the stabilizer and the sugar, whisk the sugar into the water.
Bring the mixture to a boil then cool quickly over ice.
Add the Champagne and grated zest to the syrup and churn immediately.

Champagne sorbet with green peppercorns

Ingredients

400 g (14 oz/2 cups) sugar
400 ml (14 fl oz) water
75 cl (1 bottle/3 cups) dry Champagne
5 g (1/6 oz) stabilizer
15-20 g (1/2 oz) green peppercorns in brine

Procedure

Mix the stabilizer with the sugar, whisk the sugar into the water.
Bring the mixture to a boil then cool quickly over ice.
Add the Champagne and churn immediately.
Drain the green peppercorns and stir them into the churned sorbet.
Note: This sorbet could be served at the beginning of the meal as an «aperitif».

Sorbet made with Marc de Bourgogne and Cassis

Ingredients

400 g (14 oz/2 cups) sugar
400 ml (14 fl oz) water
75 ml (1/3 cup) Marc
5 g (1/6 oz) stabilizer
500 ml (2 cups) black currant («cassis») syrup

Procedure

Mix the stabilizer with the sugar, whisk the sugar into the water.
Bring to a boil then cool quickly over ice.
Add the Marc de Bourgogne and the black currant syrup and churn immediatley.
Macerated black currant berries can be stirred into the finished sorbet.

Note: This would be a refreshing sorbet to serve as a digestif in the middle of a many course meal.

Orange sorbet with vodka

Ingredients

400 g (14 oz/2 cups) sugar
400 ml (14 fl oz) water
75 cl (3 cups) vodka
5 g (1/6 oz) stabilizer
500 ml (2 cups) orange juice

Procedure

Mix the stabilizer with the sugar, whisk the sugar into the water.
Bring to a boil then cool quickly over ice.
Add the vodka and churn immediately.

Note: This sorbet could be served at the beginning, middle or end of a meal.

Port sorbet

Ingredients

350 (12 oz) sugar
400 ml (14 fl oz) water
75 cl (3 cups) Port
5 g (1/6 oz) stabilizer

Procedure

Mix the stabilizer with the sugar. Whisk the sugar into the water.

Bring the mixture to a boil then cool quickly over ice.
Add the wine then churn immediately.
Note: In France, small cantaloupes are often served with Port poured into the hollow of a melon cut in half. The same taste combination can be achieved by serving two sorbets made of Port and cantaloupe or serve a scoop of this Port sorbet with fresh cantaloupe.

Sangria sorbet

Ingredients

1 L (1 qt) sangria

Procedure

Check the density of the sangria. Add sugar or water to achieve 1147 D then churn in an ice cream maker.

Cider sorbet

1 L (1 qt) hard cider
400 g (2 cups) sugar
300 ml (10 fl oz) water
7,5 g (1/4 oz) stabilizer
Juice of 2 lemons

Wine sorbet

1 bottle good quality red wine
500 ml (2 cups) water
450 g (2 1/4 cups) sugar
Juice of 2 lemons
Juice of 1 orange
12 g (1/3 oz) stabilizer

« Marc » parfait

12 egg yolks
250 ml (1 cup) water
250 g (8 oz/2 1/2 cups) sugar
750 ml (3 cups) heavy cream
125 ml (1/2 cup) Marc
(Marc is a strong alcohol distilled from grape skins)

Sorbets made with flowers and plants

Verveine (lime flower) sorbet

Ingredients

400 g (14 oz/2 cups) sugar
1 L (1 qt) water
10-15 g (1/2 oz) dried flowers or leaves
5 g (1/6 oz) stabilizer
1 lemon (optional)

Procedure

Infuse the dried flowers or leaves in the water (bring water to a boil add plants, cover and allow to cool to room temperature.)
Whisk in the sugar and stabilizer.
Check the density then churn in an ice cream maker.

Note: To augment the taste, flavorings such as rose water or liqueurs that compliment the flower or plant can be added.

Same procedure for :

Camomille sorbet

Lavander sorbet

Mint sorbet

Rose petal sorbet

Tea sorbet

Ice creams

Almond ice cream

Ingredients

1 L (1 qt) milk
250 ml (1 cup) heavy cream
250 g (8 oz) sugar
8 egg yolks (150 g (5 oz))
30 g (1 oz) trimoline
5 g (1/6 oz) stabilizer
300 g (10 oz) blanched almonds

Procedure

Chop the almonds. Bring the milk to a boil, add the almonds, cover and cool to room temperature then refrigerate 24 hours.
Pour the milk through a sieve, pressing on the almonds to extract flavor.
Measure the milk and add enough to make 1 litre (1 qt).
Bring the milk to a simmer with the cream and a little of the sugar.
Whisk the egg yolks until thick with the remaining sugar, trimoline and stabilizer.
Whisk a little of the hot milk into the egg yolk mixture.
Off the heat, stir the egg yolks back into the hot milk.
Return to low heat and stir until the custard coats the spoon and reaches 85 F (185 F).
Strain, cool quickly over ice, then cover and refrigerate several hours before churning.

Star anise ice cream

Ingredients

1 L (1 qt) milk
250 ml (1 cup) heavy cream
250 g (8 oz) sugar
8 egg yolks (150 g (5 oz))
30 g (1 oz) trimoline
5 g (1/6 oz) stabilizer
2-3 star anise

Procedure

Bring the milk to a boil with the cream, a little sugar and the star anise. Remove from the heat, cover and set aside to infuse.
Whisk the egg yolks until thick with the remaining sugar, trimoline and stabilizer.
Stir a little of the hot milk into the beaten egg yolks, then stir the mixture back into the hot milk.
Return to low heat and stir until the custard thickens enough to coat a spoon and reaches 85 C (185 F).
Strain, cool quickly over ice then cover and refrigerate several hours before churning.

Peanut ice cream

Ingredients

1 L (1 qt) milk
250 ml (1 cup) heavy cream
250 g (8 oz) sugar
8 egg yolks (150 g (5 oz))
30 g (1 oz) trimoline
5 g (1/6 oz) stabilizer
300 g (10 oz) roasted peanuts

Procedure

Chop the peanuts. Bring the milk to a boil, add the peanuts, cool to room temperature then cover and refrigerate 24 hours.
Pour through a sieve and press on the nuts to extract flavor.
Measure the milk and add enough to make 1 litre (1 qt).
Bring the milk to a boil with the cream and a little sugar.
Whisk the egg yolks until thick with the remaining sugar, trimoline and stabilizer.
Stir a little of the hot milk into the egg yolk mixture, then stir it back into the hot milk.
Return to low heat and stir until the the custard thickens enough to coat a spoon and reaches 85 C (185 F).
Strain, cool quickly over ice then cover and refrigerate several hours before churning.

Coffee ice cream

Ingredients

1 L (1 qt) milk
250 ml (1 cup) heavy cream
250 g (8 oz) sugar
8 egg yolks (150 g 5 oz))
30 g (1 oz) trimoline
5 g (1/6 oz) stabilizer
25 g (scant 1 oz) instant coffee
2-3 coffee beans, crushed

Procedure

Bring the milk to a boil with the coffee beans, remove from the heat , cool then cover and refrigerate 24 hours.
Pour through a sieve and add enough milk to make 1 litre (1 qt).
Bring the milk to a boil with the cream, a little sugar and the instant coffee.
Meanwhile, whisk the egg yolks until thick with the remaining sugar, trimoline and stabilizer.
Stir a little hot milk into the egg yolks then stir it back into the hot milk.
Return the custard to low heat, stirring until it thickens enough to coat a spoon and reaches 85 C (185 F).
Cool quickly over ice, cover and refrigerate several hours before churning.

Calisson ice cream

(«Calissons» are French candies made with almond paste and candied fruits from the southern French region of Provence.)

Ingredients

1 L (1 qt) milk
250 ml (1 cup) heavy cream
250 g (8 oz) sugar
8 egg yolks(150 g (5 oz))
30 g (1 oz) trimolone
5 g (1/6 oz) stabilizer
300 g (10 oz) calisson candies
(use almond paste and candied orange peel)

Procedure

Bring the milk to a boil and add the flavoring.
Cool then cover and refrigerate 24 hours.
Pour the milk through a sieve, add milk to make 1 litre (1 qt).
Bring the milk to a boil with the cream and a little sugar.
Meanwhile, whisk the egg yolks until thick with the remaining sugar, trimoline and stabilizer.
Stir a little of the hot milk into the egg yolks then pour it back into the hot milk.
Stir until the custard thickens enough to coat a spoon and reaches 85 C (185 F).
Cool quickly over ice then cover and refrigerate several hours before churning.

Note: Small chunks of the calisson candies can be added when the ice cream is churned.

Cinnamon ice cream

Ingredients

1 L (1 qt) milk
250 ml (1 cup) heavy cream
250 g (8 oz) sugar
8 egg yolks (150 g (5 oz))
30 g (1 oz) trimoline
5 g (1/6 oz) stabilizer
2-3 cinnamon sticks

Procedure

Bring the milk to a boil with the cream, a little sugar and the cinnamon sticks, set aside to infuse.
Whisk the egg yolks until thick with the remaining sugar, trimoline and stabilizer.
Return the milk to a simmer, whisk a little of the hot milk into the egg yolks then stir back into the milk.
Return to low heat and stir until the custard thickens enought to coat a spoon and reaches 85 C (185 F).
Cool quickly over ice then cover and refrigerate several hours before churning.

Ice creams (continuation)

Chocolate ice cream

Ingredients

1 L (1 qt) milk)
250 ml (1 cup) heavy cream
250 g (8 oz) sugar
8 egg yolks (150 g (5 oz))
30 g (1 oz) trimoline
5 g (1/6 oz) stabilizer
250 g (8 oz) bittersweet chocolate
5 g (1/5 oz) instant coffee

Procedure

Bring the milk to a boil with the cream and a little sugar.
Whisk the egg yolks until thick with the remaining sugar, trimoline and stabilizer.
Stir a little of the hot milk into the egg yolks then stir back into the hot milk.
Return to low heat and stir until the custard thickens enough to coat a spoon and reaches 85 C (185 F).
Off the heat, add the chocolate (chopped) and the instant coffee and stir until smooth.
Cool quickly over ice then cover and refrigerate several hours before churning.

Citronella ice cream

Ingredients

1 L (1qt) milk
250 ml (1 cup) heavy cream
250 g (8 oz) sugar
8 egg yolks150 g (5 oz)
30 g (1 oz) trimoline
5 g (1/6 oz) stabilizer
100 g (3 1/2 oz) fresh citronella
(a member of mint family with strong lemon scent)

Procedure

Bring the milk to a boil add the citronella, cool to room temperature then cover and refrigerate 24 hours.
Strain the milk, press on the citronella to extract flavor.
Add enough milk to make 1 litre (1 qt).
Bring the milk to a boil with the cream and a little sugar.
Meanwhile, whisk the egg yoks until thick with the remaining sugar, trimoline and the stabilizer.
Stir a little of the hot milk into the egg yolks then stir it back into the milk. Return to low heat and stir until the custard thickens enough to coat a spoon and reaches 85 C (185 F).
Cool quickly over ice, cover and refrigerate several hours before churning.

Date ice cream

Ingredients

1 L (1 qt) milk
250 ml (1 cup) heavy cream
250 g (8 oz) sugar
8 egg yolks (150 g (5 oz))
30 g (1 oz) trimoline
5 g (1/6 oz) stabilizer
250 g (8 oz) dried dates, chopped

Procedure

Bring the milk to a boil with the dried dates, cool then cover and refrigerate 24 hours.
Strain and press on the dates to extract flavor.
Add milk to make 1 litre (1 qt).
Bring the milk to a boil with the cream and a little sugar.
Meanwhile, whisk the egg yolks until thick with the remaining sugar, trimoline and stabilizer.
Stir a little hot milk into the egg yolks then stir back into the hot milk. Return to low heat and stir until the custard thickens enough to coat a spoon and reaches 85 C (185 F).
Cool quickly over ice, cover and refrigerate several hours before churning.

Fig ice cream

Ingredients

1 L (1 qt) milk
250 ml (1 cup) heavy cream
250 g (8 oz) sugar
8 egg yolks (150 g (5 oz))
30 g (1 oz) trimoline
5 g (1/6 oz) stabilizer
200 g (7 oz) dried figs, chopped

Procedure

Bring the milk to a boil and add the chopped figs. Cool then cover and refrigerate 24 hours.
Strain the milk, press on the dates to extract flavor, add enough milk to make 1 litre (1 qt).
Bring the milk to a boil with the cream and a little sugar.
Meanwhile, beat the egg yolks unitl thick and lemon-colored with the remaining sugar, trimoline and stabilizer.
Stir a little hot milk into the egg yolks then stir back into the hot milk.
Return to low heat and stir until the custard thickens enough to coat a spoon and reaches 85 C (185 F).
Strain, cool quickly over ice then cover and refrigerate several hours before churning.

Ginger ice cream

Ingredients

1 L (1 qt) milk
250 ml (1 cup) heavy cream
250 g (8 oz) sugar
8 egg yolks (150 g (5 oz))
30 g (1oz) trimoline
5 g (1/6 oz) stabilizer
20 g (2/3 oz) fresh gingerroot

Procedure

Bring the milk to a boil and add the the gingerroot cut into small pieces. Cover and refrigerate 24 hours.

Strain, press on the gingerroot to extract flavor then add milk to make 1 litre (1 qt).
Bring the milk to a simmer with the cream and a little sugar.
Meanwhile, beat the egg yolks until thick with the remaining sugar, trimoline and stabilizer.
Stir a little of the hot milk into the egg yolks then stir back into the hot milk.
Return to low heat and stir until the custard thickens enough to coat a spoon and reaches 85 C (185 F).
Strain, cool quickly over ice then cover and refrigerate several hours before churning.

Chestnut ice cream

Ingredients

1 L (1 qt) milk
250 ml (1 cup) heavy cream
250 g (8 oz) sugar
8 egg yolks (150 g (5 oz))
30 g (1 oz) trimoline
5 g (1/6 oz) stabilizer
250 g (8 oz) chestnut purée

Procedure

Bring the milk to a boil with the cream, a little sugar and the chestnut purée.
Meanwhile, beat the egg yolks with the remaining sugar, trimoline and stabilizer.
Stir a little hot milk into the egg yolks then stir back into the hot milk.
Return to low heat and stir until the custard reaches 85 C (185 F).
Strain, cool quickly over ice then cover and refrigeate several hours before churning.

Hazelnut ice cream

Ingredients

1 L (1 qt) milk
250 ml (1 cup) heavy cream
250 g (8 oz) sugar
8 egg yolks (150 g (5 oz))
30 g (1 oz) trimoline
5 g (1/6 oz) stabilizer
250 g (8 oz) hazelnut paste

Procedure

Bring the milk to a boil with the cream, a little sugar and the hazelnut paste.

Meanwhile beat the egg yolks until thick with the remaining sugar, trimoline and stabilizer.

Stir a little hot milk into the egg yolks then stir back into the hot milk.

Return to low heat and stir until the custard heats to 85 C (185 F).

Strain, cool quickly over ice then cover and refrigerate several hours before churning.

Walnut ice cream

Ingredients

1 L (1 qt) milk
250 ml (1 cup) heavy cream
250 g (8 oz) sugar
8 egg yolks (150 g (5 oz))
30 g (1 oz) trimoline
5 g (1/6 oz) stabilizer
250 g (8 oz) walnut paste

Procedure

Bring the milk to a boil with the cream, a little sugar and the walnut paste.

Meanwhile, beat the egg yolks until thick with the remaining sugar, trimoline and stabilizer.

Stir a little hot milk into the egg yolks then stir it back into the hot milk.

Return to low heat and stir until the custard reaches 85 C (185 F).

Strain and cool quickly over ice. Cover and refrigerate several hours before churning.

Coconut ice cream

Ingredients

1 L (1 qt) milk
250 ml (1 cup) heavy cream
250 g (8 oz) sugar
8 egg yolks (150 g (5 oz))
30 g (1 oz) trimoline
5 g (1/6 oz) stabilizer
200 g (7 oz) freshly grated coconut
Passer au chinois.
Laisser maturer au frais (+ 4°C).
Turbiner.

Procedure

Bring the milk to a boil, remove from the heat then add the grated coconut. Cool then cover and refrigerate 24 hours.

Strain then add milk to make1 litre (1 qt).

Bring the milk to a simmer with the cream and a little sugar.

Meanwhile, beat the egg yolks until thick with the remaining sugar, trimoline and stabilizer.

Stir a little hot milk into the eggs then stir back into the milk.

Return to low heat and stir until the custard heats to 85 C (185 F).

Strain then cool quickly over ice.

Cover and refrigerate several hours before churning.

Pistachio ice cream

Ingredients

1 L (1 qt) milk
250 ml (1 cup) heavy cream
250 g (8 oz) sugar
8 egg yolks (150 g (5 oz))
30 g (1 oz) trimoline
5 g (1/6 oz) stabilizer
250 g (8 oz) pistachio paste

Procedure

Bring the milk to a boil with the cream, a little sugar and the pistachio paste.

Meanwhile, beat the egg yolks until thick with the remaining sugar, trimoline and stabilizer.

Stir a little hot milk into the egg yolks then stir back into the hot milk.

Return to low heat and stir until the custard reaches 85 C (185 F).

Strain and cool quickly over ice.

Cover and refrigerate several hours before churning.

«Plombières» ice cream (vanilla with candied fruits and praline)

Ingredients

1 L (1 qt) milk
250 ml (1 cup) heavy cream
250 g (8 oz) sugar
8 egg yolks (150 g (5 oz))
50 g (1 2/3 oz) trimoline
5 g (1/6 oz) stabilizer
2 vanilla beans, split
200 g (7 oz) candied fruits, chopped
80 g (2 2/3 oz) praline, chopped
120 ml (scant 1/2 cup) Kirsch

Procedure

Macerate the chopped fruits in the Kirsch.

Bring the milk to a boil with the cream, a little sugar and the split vanilla beans.

Meanwhile, beat the egg yolks until thick with the remaining sugar, trimoline and stabilizer.

Stir a little hot milk into the egg yolks then stir back into the hot milk.

Return to low heat and stir as the custard reaches 85 C (185 F).

Strain and cool quickly over ice.

Cover and refrigerate several hours before churning.

Add the macerated fruits, Kirsch and chopped praline to the mixture when it is churned.

Praline ice cream

Ingredients

1 L (1 qt) milk
250 ml (1 cip) heavy cream
250 g (8 oz) sugar
8 egg yolks (150 g (1 oz))
30 g (1 oz) trimoline
5 g (1/6 oz) stabilizer
250 g (8 oz) praline paste
(almond brittle, ground to a paste)

Procedure

Bring the milk to a boil with the cream, a little sugar and the praline paste.

Meanwhile, beat the egg yolks until thick with the remaining sugar, trimoline and the stabilizer.

Stir a little of the hot milk into the egg yolks then stir back into the hot milk.

Return to low heat and stir until the custard reaches 85 C (185 F).

Strain and cool quickly over ice.

Cover and refrigerate several hours before churning.

Prune ice cream

Ingredients

1 L (1 qt) milk
250 ml (1 cup) heavy cream
250 g (8 oz) sugar
8 egg yolks (150 g (5 oz))
30 g (1 ozz) trimoline
5 g (1/6 oz) stabilizer
200 g (7 oz) prunes, chopped

Procedure

Bring the milk to a boil, add the chopped prunes. When cooled slightly, cover and refrigerate 24 hours.

Strain the milk, press on the prunes to extract flavor, and bring to a simmer with the cream and a little sugar.

Meanwhile, beat the egg yolks until thick with the remaining sugar, trimoline and stabilizer.

Stir a little hot milk into the eggs then stir back into the hot milk.

Return to low heat, stirring as the custard reaches 85 C (185 F).

Strain and cool quickly over ice. Cover and refrigerate several hours before churning.

Vanilla ice cream

Ingredients

1 L (1 qt) milk
250 ml (1 cup) heavy cream
250 g (8 oz) sugar
8 egg yolks (150 g (5 oz))
30 g (1 oz) trimoline
5 g (1/6 oz) stabilizer
2 vanilla beans, split

Procedure

Bring the milk to a boil with the cream, vanilla beans and a little sugar.

Meanwhile, beat the egg yolks unitl thick with the remaining sugar, trimoline and stabilizer.

Stir a little of the hot milk into the eggs then stir back into the hot milk.

Retun to low heat and stir until the custard thickens enough to coat a spoon and reaches 85 C (185 F).

Strain and cool quickly over ice.

Cover and refrigerate several hours to allow the flavor to develop before churning.

Pastries to serve with ice cream

Cream puff dough («pâte à choux»)

Ingredients

250 ml (1 cup) water
200 g (7 oz) flour
100 g (3 1/2 oz) butter
5 g (1 tsp) salt
6 eggs

Procedure

Bring the water to a boil with the butter and the salt.
Off the heat, add the flour all at once and stir to blend. Return to low heat and stir to dry out the mixture a little.
Off the heat, beat in the eggs one at a time.
Pipe the batter in the desired size on lightly buttered baking sheets.
Bake at 200 C (400 F).

Genoise sponge cake

Ingredients

8 large eggs
250 g (8 oz) sugar
250 g (8 oz) flour
Butter and flour for the molds

Procedure

Brush softened butter on the molds, dust with flour and shake off the excess.
Whisk the eggs over low heat or a water bath to warm them to about 40 C (110 F).
Off the heat, beat the warmed eggs until very thick, lemon-colored and form a ribbon of batter when the whisk is lifted.
Sift the flour onto the egg mixture and gently incorporate.
Transfer to the mold immediately and bake in a preheated oven, 190 C (375 F).

172

Chocolate genoise

Ingredients

8 large eggs
250 g (8 oz) sugar
225 g (7 3/4 oz) flour
40 g (1 1/3 oz) cocoa powder

Procedure

Same as for plain genoise. Sift the flour and cocoa powder together before sifting into the eggs.

Italian meringue

Ingredients

1 L (1 qt) egg whites
2 kg (4 lbs) sugar

Procedure

Beat the egg whites to soft peaks.
Meanwhile, cook the sugar with a little water to the soft ball stage (115 C (238 F)).
With the mixer on high speed, pour the hot syrup slowly into the egg whites and continue to beat until cool.

Swiss meringue

Ingredients

1 L (1 qt) egg whites
1 kg (2 lbs) granulated sugar
1 kg (2 lbs) powdered sugar

Procedure

Beat the eggs to firm peaks with the granulated sugar.
Gently mix in the powdered sugar (sifted) by hand.
Pipe the meringue on lightly buttered and floured baking sheets. Bake about 3 hours at 100 C (210 F).

Almond sponge cake

Ingredients

450 g (15 oz) almond paste
6 eggs
8 egg whites
80 g (2 2/3 oz) sugar
60 g (2 oz) flour

Procedure

Beat the almond paste and eggs until smooth.
Beat the egg whites to firm peaks with the sugar.
Blend the flour into the almond paste mixture then gently fold in the meringue.
Transfer the batter to baking sheets lined with parchment paper.
Bake in a preheated oven, 210 C (425 F).

Sweet pie pastry («pâte sucrée»)

Ingredients

500 g (1 lb) flour
200 g (7 oz) powdered sugar
200 g (7 oz) butter
2 eggs
1/2 tsp vanilla extract

Procedure

Beat the butter and sugar until light and creamy, beat in the eggs and vanilla.
Stir in the flour to make a soft dough.
Cover and refrigerate until firm, roll out and use as needed.

Almond butter cookies

Cream 200 g (7oz) butter.
Beat in 200 g (7 oz) almond paste, a little vanilla and 1 egg.
Stir in 280 g (9 oz) flour.
Pipe onto a buttered baking sheet and bake at 180 C (360 F).

Coconut «tuiles» cookies

Mix 250 g (8 oz) with 300 g (10 oz) sugar.
Stir in 250 ml (1 cup) egg whites.
Blend in 150 g (5 oz) melted butter.
Blend in 50 g (1 2/3 oz) flour.
Spoon mounds of batter on well buttered baking sheets.
Flatten the batter with a fork and bake at 180 C (360 F).
Form the cookies while still warm in a traditional «tuiles» pan or over a rolling pin to make the curved «tile» or «tuile» shape.
Serve plain or glazed with covering chocolate.

Almond «tuiles»

Mix 250 g (8 oz) toasted, sliced almonds with 250 g (8 oz) powdered sugar and 25 g (scant 1 oz) flour.
Stir in 6 egg whites and 50 g (1 2/3 oz) melted butter.
Spoon mounds of batter on well buttered baking sheets.
Flatten the batter with a fork and bake at 180 C (360 F).
Form the cookies as described in «coconut tuiles».
Serve plain or glazed with covering chocolate.

Almond treats

In a food processor, grind 500 g (1 lb) blanched almonds with 250 g (8 oz) sugar.
Stir in enough egg whites to make smooth paste.
Pipe in a pretty design with piping bag on parchment paper-lined baking sheets.
Bake at 200 C (400 F) a few minutes, until lightly browned.

Marzipan candies

Blend equal weights powdered sugar with almond paste or use ready-made marzipan.
Lemon: For 2 lbs, add the grated zest of 3 lemons and yellow food coloring, Form into small lemon shapes.
Cherry: Add chopped candied cherries, form into small balls and roll in powdered sugar.
Hazelnut: Add green food coloring. Roll a bit of marzipan around a toasted hazelnut.

Lemon sugar cookies

Cream 200 g (7 oz) butter with 100 g (3 1/2 oz) sugar and 2 egg whites.
Stir in 250 g (8 oz) flour, a pinch of salt and the zest of 2 lemons.
Form the dough into rolls about 2.5 cm (1 inch) across, cover and chill until firm.
Roll the chilled dough in sugar then cut slices about 4 mm (1/6 inch).
Bake at 180 C (360 F) about 5 minutes.

Raisin cookies

Cream 250 g (8 oz) butter.
Blend in 250 g (8 oz) powdered sugar.
Blend in 5 eggs, one at a time.
Blend in 400 g (14 oz) flour, 200 g (7 oz) raisins and a pinch of salt.
Spoon small mounds of batter on buttered baking sheets and bake at 180 C (360 F).

"Napolitains"

Heat 300 g (10 oz) butter unitl it melts and turns a nutty brown color, set aside.
In a food processor, grind together 250 g (8 oz) blanched almonds, 150 g (5 oz) walnuts, and 250 g (8 oz) sugar.
Blend in 8 egg whites and 75 g (2 1/2 oz) cornstarch.
Blend in the butter and 75 g (2 1/2 oz) honey.
Transfer the batter to small buttered molds and bake at 180 C (360 F).

"Biarritz"

In a food processor, grind together 250 g (8 oz) each hazelnuts and sugar.
Stir in 200 g (7 oz) flour, 200 ml (7 fl oz) milk and 250 g (8 oz) melted butter.
Fold in 120 g (scant 4 oz) egg whites, beaten to firm peaks.
Spoon the batter onto buttered baking sheets.
Bake at 180 C (360 F).
Glaze the cooled cookies with covering chocolate.

"Massepains"

In a food processor, grind 250 g (8 oz) blanched almonds with 150 g (5 oz) sugar. Stir in the grated zest of 2 lemons.
Beat 200 g (7 oz) egg whites to firm peaks with 50 g (1/4 cup) sugar.
Gently fold the beaten egg whites into the almond mixture.
Pipe small mounds on heavy duty (or doubled) baking sheets lined with parchment paper.
Bake in a convection oven at 180 C (360 F) until lightly browned.
Sandwich two cookies together with raspberry jam or lemon buttercream.

"Doras"

Cream 250 g (8 oz) butter.
Add 500 g (1 lb) almond paste and 10 egg whites and blend until smooth.
Stir in 300 g (10 oz) flour.
Pipe onto floured (for «Doras») or buttered baking sheets (for «Biarritz).
Bake at 180 C (360 F).
To make «Doras», sandwich two cookies together with praline buttercream. To make Biarritz, glaze with chocolate.

Black currant tartlettes

Line bite-size tart molds with thin rounds of puff pastry (this is a good use for scraps of dough).
Pipe a little almond cream (equal weights ground almonds, sugar, butter, eggs) into each mold.
Add a few fresh (or canned) black or red currants to each. Place a very thin circle of puff pastry on top, seal the edges and glaze with egg wash.
Sprinkle the top with sliced almonds and bake at 180 C (360 F) about 15 minutes or until lightly browned.

Pineapple cakes

In a mixer, blend 250 g (8 oz) almond paste with 30 g (1 oz) apricot purée, 2 eggs and 1 egg yolk until smooth.
Stir in 25 g (scant 1 oz) flour and 60 g (2 oz) melted butter.
Pipe the batter into small muffin tins with paper cupcake liners.
Place a small piece of fresh, poached pineapple on top of each cake.
Bake at 180 C (360 F) until lightly browned.

"Rothschilds"

Beat 250 ml (1 cup) egg whites to firm peaks with 60 g (2 oz) sugar.
Beat 300 g (10 oz) almond paste until smooth.
Fold in the beaten egg whites and 50 g (1 2/3 oz) flour.
Pipe the batter onto buttered and floured baking sheets.
Bake at 180 C (360 F).
Glaze with covering chocolate («Rothschilds»), or sandwich two cookies together with raspberry jam or currant jelly ("Eponges").

«Visitandines»

In a food processor, grind together150 g (5 oz) blanched almonds and 200 g (7 oz/1 cup) sugar.
Stir in 4 egg whites and the grated zest of 1 lemon.
Stir in 75 g (2 1/2 oz) flour and 200 g (7 oz) browned butter.
Pipe the mixture into small buttered molds (the traditional «visitandine molds are «boat-shaped»).
Bake at 180 C (360 F).
Serve plain or glazed with lemon fondant.

Grand Marnier cakes

In a mixer, blend 450 g (15 oz) almond paste with 230 g (7 1/2 oz) eggs until smooth.
Blend in 115 g (3 3/4 oz) melted butter.
Transfer the batter to a jelly roll pan 40 X 60 cm (16 X 24 in) lined with parchment paper.
Bake at 170 C (350 F) until set.
Fresh from the oven, moisten the cake with 3/4 cup sugar syrup flavored with 25 ml (2/3 fl oz) Grand Marnier.
Unmold and place in the freezer.
Glaze one side with covering chocolate, chill to set then turn over and glaze the other side.
Cut into small squares.

Cookies made with puff pastry
Puff pastry for cookies

Blend 500 g (1 lb) flour with 10 g (2 tsp) salt and 75 g (2 1/2 oz) cold butter.
Stir in 250 ml (1 cup) cold water and 2 egg yolks to make a firm, smooth dough.
Form into a ball, roll on a floured surface into a circle and place 400 g (14 oz) unsalted butter in the center. Fold the edges of the dough over the butter, and overlap the edges. Turn the package over and roll into a rectangle. Fold into thirds. Turn the square of dough so that the open ends are north and south, roll out and fold into thirds again. Cover and refrigerate 15 minutes. Repeat the rolling, folding and turning process 4 times, letting the dough rest after two «turns.» Note: Since these pastries do not expand as much as «patty shells», unflavored trimmings from other batches of puff pastry can be placed in the center of the rectangle on the fifth turn.

Match sticks

Roll out a sheet of chilled puff pastry to about 3 mm (1/8 in), chill until firm, then brush with royal icing (powdered sugar with egg whites.)
Cut the pastry into rectangles 4 X 2 cm (1 1/2 X 3/4 in.)
Transfer the strips to a baking sheet lined with dampened parchment paper.
Bake in a convection oven at 180-200 C (375-400 F) about 15 minutes or until puffed and lightly browned.

"Palmiers" ("elephant ears")

Take a batch of chilled puff pastry, open the folds and cover the rectangle of dough with granulated sugar and refold into thirds. Do not do a «turn» of the puff pastry with sugar on the work surface as it will not puff as well and will become hard when baked.
Roll out the dough to about 3 mm (1/8 in) with a little sugar on the work surface.
Fold over the edges of the dough about 11/2 in and fold over each side again to meet in the middle, then fold the two folded sides on top of each other like a book. Chill the dough, sprinkle some sugar on the cutting board and cut strips about 5 mm (1/4 in.)
Lay the cookies flat on a parchment-lined baking sheet. Bake at 180-200C (375-400 F) about 10-15 minutes or until golden brown.

"Papillons" (butterflies)

Open the folds of a chilled batch of puff pastry and cover the rectangle of dough with granulated sugar.
Like the palmiers, do not use sugar when «turning» the dough as it will become hard when baked.
On a work surface covered with a little sugar, roll out the dough to about 3 mm (1/8 in.)
Cut strips about 4 cm (1 1/2 in) wide. Brush the strips with a little water and pile three strips on top of each other and press gently to stick together. Cut strips from the end about 6 mm (1/4 in), pinch the middle of the layers and twist. Place the «butterflies» on parchment-lined baking sheets and bake at 180-200 C (375-400 F) about 10-15 minutes or until puffed and golden brown.

173

Sauces and «coulis» to serve with frozen desserts

Creamy or chocolate sauces and fruit purées («coulis») are used to coat some desserts or are poured on the side of the plate to add flavor and color.

Vanilla crème anglaise (custard sauce)

Ingredients

1 L (1 qt) whole milk
250 ml (1 cup) heavy cream
8 egg yolks
200 g (1 cup) sugar
30 g (1 oz) trimoline (optional)
2 vanilla beans, split

Procedure

Combine the milk, cream, vanilla beans and a little sugar, bring to a simmer, cover, infuse.
Meanwhile, whisk the egg yolks with the remaining sugar and trimoline until thick.
Whisk a little hot milk into the egg yolk mixture, then transfer it all back into the milk.
Return the pot to medium heat, stir constantly as the custard thickens enough to coat the spoon (it is pasteurized at 80 C (175 F.)
Pour through a fine-meshed strainer and cool quickly over ice, cover and refrigerate several hours before serving.

Chocolate crème anglaise

Ingredients

1 L (1 qt) whole milk
250 ml (1 cup) heavy cream
8 egg yolks
200 g (1 cup) sugar
30 g (1 oz) trimoline (optional)
200 g (7 oz) bittersweet chocolate, chopped
2 vanilla beans, split

Procedure

Bring to a simmer the milk, cream, vanilla beans and a little sugar. Add the chopped chocolate, cover and set aside to let the vanilla infuse and the chocolate melt.
Meanwhile, whisk the egg yolks with the remaining sugar and trimoline until thick.
Pour a little hot milk into the egg yolk mixture, then transfer it back into the milk.
Cook the custard over medium heat, stirring constantly until it thickens enough to coat a spoon (80 C (175 F.))
Pour through fine-meshed strainer, cool quickly over ice then cover and refrigerate several hours before using.

Chocolate Sauce

Ingredients

1 L (1 qt) whole milk
100 g (3 1/2 oz) unsalted butter
50 g (1 2/3 oz) glucose
200 g (7 oz) bittersweet chocolate (chopped)
20 ml (2/3 fl oz) rum (optional)

Procedure

Bring the milk and glucose to a boil.
Off the heat, add the butter and chocolate, stir until the chocolate melts.
Cool then stir in rum.

Black currant or passion fruit coulis

Ingredients

500 g (1 lb) fruit juice
300 g (10 oz) sugar
300 ml (10 fl oz) water
10 g (1/3 oz) glucose
Juice of 1 lemon

Procedure

Simmer the sugar, water and glucose to make a syrup.
Stir in the fruit juice.
Cool quickly over ice.
Stir in the lemon juice.

Strawberry coulis (or raspberry/pineapple)

Ingredients

500g (1 lb) fruit purée
300 g (10 oz) sugar
300 ml (10 fl oz) water
10 g (1/3 oz) glucose
Juice of 1 lemon

Procedure

Simmer the sugar, water and glucose to make a syrup.
Stir in the fruit purée.
Cool quickly over ice.
Stir in the lemon juice.

Apricot or peach coulis

Ingredients

500 g (1 lb) fruit purée
300 g (20 oz) sugar
300 ml (10 fl oz) water
10 g (1/3 oz) glucose
Juice of 1 lemon

Procedure

Simmer the sugar, water and glucose to make a syrup.
Stir in the fruit purée.
Cool quickly over ice.
Stir in the lemon juice.

Sorbets and ice creams: a marriage of flavors

Any combination of flavors is possible if the producta are well made and the intensity of flavors are balanced.
To guide your choice of flavor combinations, match regional ingredients and fruits that

are in season. Color, also, should be considered.
Of course, there are classic marriages of flavors that will always be delicious. Here are some examples of flavors that enhance each other.

It is recommended to not combine more than three flavors so that each can be tasted and enjoyed.

When combining two or three, it is best if one is a dominant flavor and the others be more discreet and enhance the first.

For example:

Principle flavor
Raspberry

Secondary flavors
Passion fruit:
Contributes a touch of acidity which enhances the sweetness of the raspberry. Be careful not to overpower the raspberry with passion fruit that is too strong.

Pistachio:
Contributes a counterpoint to the acidity of the passion fruit and the sweetness of the raspberry.

Principle flavor
Vanilla

Secondary flavors
Chocolate:
The intensity of the chocolate should not be too strong so that the vanilla and strawberry is not overpowered.

Strawberry:
Contributes a touch of acidity which enhances the other two flavors.

Another alternative is to add a sauce or fruit coulis to a frozen dessert with two flavors to add contrast in color and flavor to enhance the flavors of the ice cream, parfait and/or sorbets in the dessert.

With vanilla:

Chocolate
Raspberry
Strawberry
Praline
Hazelnut
Black currant
Caramel
Pistachio
Orange liqueur
Red currant
Rum
Kirsch

With apricot:

Red currant
Strawberry
Black currant
Raspberry
Black raspberry
Pistachio
Sweet white wine

With raspberry:

Vanilla
Pistachio
Mint
Lemon
Mango
Passion fruit
Chocolate
Pineapple
Apricot

With strawberry:

Vanilla
Lemon
Mint
Honey
Orange
Pear liqueur
Black currant
Apricot
Champagne
Sweet wine
Honey

With praline:
hazelnut, pistachio:

Raspberry
Strawberry
Black currant
Cherry
Red currant
Passion fruit
Chocolate
Vanilla

With orange:

Pineapple
Chocolate
Pistachio
Black currant
Tea
Chicory
Grenadine
Caramel
Vodka, Gin, Whiskey

With chocolate:

Vanilla
Pistachio
Praline
Hazelnut
Caramel
Raspberry
Lemon
Mint
Pineapple
Mandarine orange
Tea, plain
Tea, flavored

With pineapple:

Strawberry
Raspberry
Black currant
Orange
Mango
Papaya
Black raspberry
Chocolate
Rum

175

Components of Ice Cream

Ingredients	Purpose	Composition/source	**Amount** *per 1 L (1 qt) milk*
Milk	Milk is composed principally of water. The fat and protein in milk contribute to the texture, flavor and consistency of the finished product.	*Contains a large proportion of water (liquid portion of milk), sugars (lactose), fats (butterfat), proteins (casein, globuline??, albumin), minerals (calcium, phosphorus), vitamins (A, B2, C, D) and lactic acids (which are mostly destroyed by heat.)*	*The standard recipe for ice cream is based on one liter (one quart) milk.*
Powdered milk	Contributes substance without water to the mixture. Improves the texture of the ice cream. Helps to maintain a good texture when the ice cream is stored.	*Contains the same components as liquid milk without the water.*	*20-40 g (2/3- 1 1/3 oz) per liter (qt) milk*
Cream	Heavy cream contributes to the smooth texture and shiny appearance of ice cream. The high fat content adds flavor and volume.	*Contains the same nutrients as milk, but in higher proportions because cream has less water.*	*80-100 ml (about 3 fl oz) per L (qt) milk*
Butter (unsalted)	Same contribution as cream, in concentrated form.	*Contains mostly fat and Vitamin A.*	*40-50 g (1 1/3-1 2/3 oz)*
Egg yolks	Adds smooth texture, taste and color. Contributes to the volume. Use just enough eggs to obtain the right texture, the taste can be heavy and unpleasant if too many are used.	*Contain proteins and fat, water makes up half of the weight.*	*120-160 g (about 6-8 egg yolks)*
Sugar (saccarose)	Principle sweetener in ice cream. Sweetening capacity is 100%; all other sugars are measured against this pure form of sugar.	*In granulated form or powdered, saccarose is 100% carbohydrate and contains no water. Saccarose is made from sugar beets or sugar cane.*	*200-300 g (7-10 oz) depending on the flavoring.*
Powdered glucose	Prevents sugar crystals from forming. Too much powdered glucose can make the ice cream dry and liable to crack when scooped. Powdered glucose contains about 40% saccarose, so mixtures containing it are less sweet.	*Glucose is a carbohydrate derived from cornstarch. Like cornstarch, powdered glucose contains little or no water.*	*30-40 g (1-11/3 oz) depending on the desired texture.*
Trimoline	Very effective in preventing the formation of crystals. Trimoline softens the cooked egg yolks which tend to harden in the ice cream when frozen. Trimoline is an inverted sugar which is 20-30% sweeter than saccarose.	*Trimoline is made from saccarose made from beet sugar. It is sold as a paste or thick syrup. Whitish syrup which contains 20-30% water depending on the brand.*	*40 g (1 1/3 oz) per liter (qt) milk, or as needed*

Ingredients	Purpose	Composition/source	Amount _per 1 L (1 qt) milk_
Wine, eau de vie liqueur	Used as a flavoring. The alcohol lowers the freezing temperature of the mixture. If alcohol is added in large quantities then the amount of sugar must be reduced. Sorbets made with wines (Champagne) and liquors (vodka) are very popular as a refreshment to «cleanse one's palate» between courses of a large meal. Alcoholic beverages are made from a variety of fruits, plants and grains.	_The fermentation process converts the sugar into alcohol. Fermented liquids can then be distilled to concentrate the alcohol._	_Take into account the degree of alcohol and intensity of flavor and vary the small amounts accordingly_
Fruits and nuts	Basic ingredient of sorbets. Used as a flavoring in ice creams. Different fruits contribute various textures.	_Contain water, cellulose, sugars (glucose and fructose). Fruits contribute Vitamin C. Nuts (almonds, walnuts, hazelnuts, pistachios) contain fat._	_Quantities vary according to regulations and level of quality._
Vanilla	Most popular flavoring in ice cream making.	_Seeds of tropical plant._	_1-2 vanilla beans per liter (qt) depending on flavor desired_
Vanilla extract	Easy to use. Add directly to the mixture.	_Made by macerating the vanilla beans and extracting the flavor by centrifuge._	_Few drops per liter (qt) milk._
Cocoa powder	Adds pure taste of chocolate, always very popular. This dry powder adds concentrated flavor with no water.	_Choose pure cocoa powder with no sugar added._	_About 80-130 g (2 2/3 -4 oz) per liter (qt) milk in addition to solid chocolate._
Chocolate	Strong flavor containing sugars and fats. Used to distinctivetaste to sauces, parfaits and ice cream.	_Contains cocoa, cocoa butter and sugar Baking, eating and covering chocolates have varying amounts of cocoa butter._	_100-250 g (3 1/2-8oz) per liter (qt) milk_
Praline	Popular flavor in pastries and frozen desserts, usually made with toasted almonds. Adds more sugar to the recipe. Nut pastes, without sugar, can be used.	_Praline is 50% toasted almonds or hazelnuts and 50 % cooked sugar. Superior products contain 60 % nuts, 40% sugar._	_100-250 g (3 1/2-8 oz) per liter (qt) milk_
Coffee	Fresh ground beans infused into the liquid (milk) of the recipe. Do not boil the liquid once the coffee is added, which would alter the flavor. The color of homemade coffee ice cream will become darker as it sits in the freezer.	_Coffee flavor can be infused from freshly ground beans or added in instant form. In France, a sweetened liquid coffee concentrate is often used to flavor custards and sauces._	_Consider the form of coffee flavoring used, the desired strength of coffee flavor._
Flavorings, extracts	Can be used as principle flavor or to reinforce another flavor. Fruit mixtures often contain a flavoring to augment the taste.	_There are many extracts and flavorings to choose from. Some contain alcohol and are obtained through distillation._	_Amount used depends on regulations (for professional manufacture), strength of extract and desired flavor._

Vocabulary in French «Glacerie»

French cooking has a very precise vocabulary which makes it possible for chefs to communicate with staff quickly and efficiently. Each branch of cooking has its own lexique; here a few of the terms used in ice cream making or «glacerie.»

«Appareil» (mixture, batter)

A combination of ingredients, usually liquid (pourable) which is then cooked or combined with other ingredients to make a finished product.

«Bombe glacee»

A classic «bombe» is made with egg yolks cooked with sugar syrup («pate à bombe») blended with whipped cream (which becomes a «parfait» mixture.) It is traditionally molded in a half sphere mold. Modern bombes are sometimes made with different layers of ice cream and sorbets.

«Cartouche eutectique» (ice packs)

Metal or plastic container filled with a substance which stays frozen several hours.
«Glaciers» will use these ice packs to chill the marble work surface to facilitate the assembly of frozen desserts.
These packs also are used to maintain a low temperature in the large coolers used for transporting frozen desserts to event locations. The «cartouce» has replaced recipients filled with ice and salt, formerly used to chill the work surface.

«Chablon»

French term for a thin layer of covering chocolate brushed on the base of a dessert. Also the name for a special piping utensil used to make small cookies and decorations with melted chocolate or batter such as «pate à cornet» or cigarette batter.

«Chemiser» (to line)

To apply the first layer of a preparation by lining the inside of the mold with a thin layer of one type of ice cream, then freezing to harden before adding subsequent layers.

«Densité» (density)

The concentration of sugar in the liquid portion of a sorbet must be at just the right level in order to achieve the best texture. The level of sugar density is measured with one of two tools, the «densimetre» or «pese sirop.» One measures the water content (hygrometer) and the other measures the strength of the sugar solution.

«Enrober» (to coat, cover)

To coat a dessert with a thin sauce or covering of chocolate, either by dipping into the sauce or by pouring it over the dessert.

«Foisonnement» (increase in volume)

«Foisonnement» takes place during two stages:
* When a custard or sorbet which contains a stablizer is «maturing» in the refrigerator before churning, the stabilizer swells slightly which thickens and increases the volume of the liquid.
* During the churning process, air is incorporated into the mixture, further increasing the volume.
French legislation allows a maximum of 100% «foisonnement.»

«Frapper» (to chill, freeze)

Molds that are going to be filled with a frozen mixture are placed in the freezer to chill them so that the layer of sorbet or ice cream will adhere better and not melt.

«Ganache»

Creamy chocolate mixture (equal weights chocolate and cream; bring cream to a boil, add chopped chocolate, stir until creamy.) Used to make truffles, chocolate glaze.

«Glacer» (to glaze)

To cover a dessert with a thin shiny coat of glaze (chocolate or jam) to give it a smooth, shiny appearance.

«Infuser» (to infuse)

To flavor a liquid by adding an aromatic ingredient which releases its flavor in hot liquid.

«Interieur»

A special mold which forms a smooth impression in a layer of ice cream or sorbet so that another layer can be added.

«Macerer» (to macerate)

To soak fresh or cooked fruits in a flavorful liquid (often wine or liqueur) to flavor and soften the fruits.

«Maturer» (to «mature»)

An ice cream or sorbet mixture benefits from a «maturing» process: the cooled mixture is covered and refrigerated for up to 24 hours to allow the flavors to develop and «mature.» The stabilizer, if used, will swell and thicken the mixture during this process.

«Monter» (to beat, whip)

To lighten the texture of a mixture by beating or whipping it with a whisk which incorporates air into it.

«Mouler» (to mold)

To make a dessert in a desired shape using a mold.

«Napper» (see «glacer»)

To cover or glaze with jam or chocolate to give the preparation a shiny appearance.

«Parfait»

A French «parfait» is a creamy mixture made with egg yolk cooked with sugar syrup blended with whipped cream and flavoring (very similar to «bombe».) The classic «parfait» is molded in a conical shape.

«Pasteuriser» (to pasteurize)

To destroy micro organisms by controlled heating to a specific temperature for a set period of time. The mixture must then be chilled quickly to inhibit bacterial growth. This process is an obligatory step in making ice cream.

«Praline, Pralinettes»

Chopped almonds cooked in caramel. Praline can be ground to a paste and used to flavor milk for ice cream or parfaits, or the praline can be dropped by spoonfuls to make bite-size «pralinettes» that can be used to add texture to a mixture or to decorate the top of a finished dessert.

«Sangler» (to freeze)

Term used for «freezing», either to chill a mold or the freezing and firming process that takes place during churning.

«Surgeler» (quick, deep freeze)

Quick freezing process which drops the temperature of a finished product below -20 C (-6 F) which minimizes the formation of ice crystals. This maintains the light texture as well as the taste and color. French legislation requires that frozen products are chilled to a temperature of -20 C (-6 F) for at least 1 hour. The products can then be stored at 0 C (32 F.)
Quick freezing also minimizes the chances that bacteria will form (the temperature at which bacteria multiply does not last long enough for growth.)

«Tant pour tant» (almond paste)

Almonds and sugar blended in equal amounts to a stiff paste. Used for sponge cakes, frangipane (almond cream), to flavor meringues and to make specialty cookies.

Availability of fresh fruits in France by season

(Check the availability of fresh fruits in your region.)

Fruits	January	February	March	April	May	June	July	August	September	October	November	December
Apricots												
Pineapples												
Avocados												
Bananas												
Cherries												
Lemons												
Clementines												
Green figs												
Purple figs												
Strawberries												
Raspberries												
Kiwis												
Mandarine oranges												
Cantaloupes												
Nectarines												
"Brugnon"												
Oranges												
Watermelons												
Peaches												
Fall pears												
Summer pears												
Winter pears												
White grapefruit												
Pink grapefruit												
Red grapefruit												
Golden Delicious apples												
Granny Smith apples												
Starking apples												
Plums												
Grapes												

Additional information to previous Chapters

P. 12 - Tools and equipment

Molds used for making ice cream

Among the classic molds used in France are the following:

- *Square molds:* With or without decoration in sizes that range from 1/4 L (about 1 cup) to 1.5 L (about 6 cups.) Frozen desserts made in these molds are often made ahead for "take out" (the molds are often sold as "les moules à glace portative»).

- *"Plombières" mold:* Cylindrical, also used for "take out" and for original desserts.

- *"Bombe" mold:* Usually a half sphere or oblong, very easy to unmold.

- *"Parfait" mold:* Conical with smooth or diamond relief design. This mold is used less in shops because the shape requires special packaging.

- *Fruit and dove molds:* The flavor of the sorbet can match the fruit-shaped mold and birds can be made in an array of bright colors.

- *Brick-shaped mold or "napolitaine»:* Long loaf-shaped pan with a sliding cover, often used for multi-layered desserts and frozen nougat. Easy to serve neat square slices, cut from the end.

- *Ice cream bar mold* («moules à sucettes glacées»): Designed to mold individual servings of ice cream on a stick, usually coated in chocolate.

- *Rings and square forms:* Stainless steel forms that are placed on a parchment lined baking sheet. Multi-layered desserts are quickly assembled in the forms which are then heated with a blow torch and easily lifted off the dessert.

- *Soufflé mold:* Used for sweet and savory hot soufflés. For cold and frozen soufflés, a strip of parchment paper can be wrapped around the mold and attached with string to form a "collar" then the mixture is added to the top of the collar for a dramatic effect.

- *Personalized molds:* With a special machine which heats plastic around a variety of forms, personalized molds can be made for any occasion. This technology is only used by large-scale manufacturers that can afford the equipment.

P. 28- "Colombe" Sundae

The cookie dove

Make a template of a dove, cut from a sheet of thick plastic. Beat together 500 g (1 lb) almond paste and 3-4 egg whites to make a batter (enough to make 2-3 dozen depending on size).

Spread the batter over the template onto a baking sheet that is either lined with parchment paper or heavily buttered and chilled. Bake in a hot oven (200-220 C (400-425 F)) until lightly browned.

With a spatula, transfer the doves to a cooling rack as soon as they are cooked.

P. 47 - Ice base for a frozen centerpiece

Advice

If you have made your own block of ice, be sure to remove it from the freezer at least one hour (depending on the size) before you plan to sculpt the finishing touches. Warming the ice slightly at room temperature closes the fissures that form when the water is frozen which could cause large cracks if the ice is worked straight from the freezer. Do not place the ice under cold running water. Be sure that the sculpting tools are well sharpened.

Procedure

Illustration 1 :
Fill a cylindrical recipient with cold water. Place in the sub zero freezer several days, then unmold.

Illustration 2 :
Trace the form of the base on the side of the ice with a V-shaped tool.

Illustration 3 :
Cut around the "cup" of the base with a flat 40 mm (1 1/2 inch) cutting tool. Trace a smaller cylinder on top of the first which will form the "foot" of the base.

Illustration 4 :
Chip down to the flat bottom of the base and chip around the rounded portion with the V-shaped tool.

Illustration 5 :
With a rounded cutting tool, hollow out the base and with the V-shaped tool, form the decorative border.

Illustration 6 :
Assemble the scoops of ice cream or profiteroles on the base in a dramatic pyramid shape and decorate with birds or flowers made from cookies (pâte à cornet).

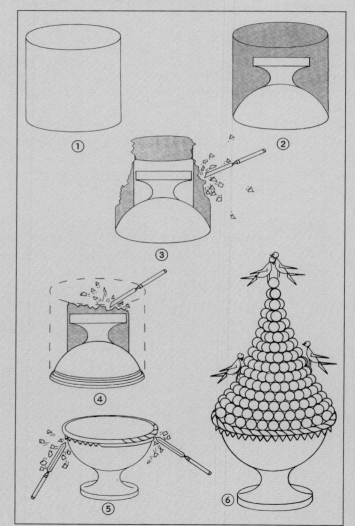

Equipment for Making Frozen Desserts

Know how to choose and use equipment

Well made ice cream, sorbets and parfait are a result of a precise process comprising many steps.
Machines, made for a specific purpose, enables the chef to execute these steps with exactitude.
In France, where fresh breads, pastries and frozen desserts are made for the public by individuals and small scale producers as well as on an industrial scale, machines have been developed in various sizes to adapt to the wide range of needs.

Contents

A. Small tools

Many of the tools used for cuisine and pastry making, such as wooden spoons, plastic scrapers, bowls, etc. are also used by the «glacier.» In many cases, there is an overlap between the work of the pastry maker and «glacier»; many frozen desserts have a cake base and are sold in pastry shops. The introduction of this book details tools particular to the «glacier».

B. Professional equipment

Professional equipment is designed to give high quality, hygienic and consistent results.
The three machines needed in large scale ice cream making are detailed on the following pages:
- Pasteurizer
- Churn
- Multi-function machine

Note from the Editor

In order to describe the functions of these machines, the editor has collaborated with the AUTOFRIGOR Company which manufactures and distributes equipment for the «glacerie» trade in France and throughout Europe.

For 75 years, AUTOFRIGOR has produced high quality equipment, always updating their machines to keep up with the many advancements in the field of frozen confections.

A logical process

Before choosing equipment, there are many things to consider.
The type of ingredients used, and the precise steps of making ice cream and sorbets.
Each step is important and the kitchen must be equipped to accomplish each step.

1. *Choosing and storing ingredients.*

2. *Precise measurement of ingredients and preliminary preparation.*

3. *Pasteurizing*

4. *Homogenizing*

5. *«Maturing»*

6. *Churning*

7. *Deep freezing and storage*

Know how to choose and use equipment - Step by Step Techniques

1. Choosing ingredients

This first step in the process determines the quality of the finished product: fresh, flavorful products make high quality, delicious frozen desserts. Buy seasonal products to get quality at a reasonable price.

2. Measuring ingredients and preliminary preparation

Weighing and measuring accurately insures the consistent quality every time. Ingredients which have a strong flavor or that effect the texture must be measured precisely and used with great care. If using stabilizers, for example, check the recommended dose for the volume you are making, adding too much could ruin the product.

Be aware of the fat content of dairy products and the sugar content of fruits and make minor adjustments where needed to achieve the best taste and texture.

3. Pasteurizing

Pasteurizing has three benefits when making frozen desserts:

• Destroys germs and bacteria.
• Minimizes the formation of bacteria during the cooling process.
• The controlled heating process used to pasteurize an ice cream mixture also coagulates the protein in the egg yolks, making a thick, smooth mixture. The increase in volume at this stage makes the ice cream light and rich at the same time.

Pasteur's discovery that bacteria multiply most quickly between 15-45 C (50-125 F) led to the process which heats the mixture quickly past the «danger zone» then cools it quickly. Bacteria will multiply every 15 minutes if left too long at the tepid temperature in between.

On a small scale, pasteurizing can be done on a stove in a heavy pot with a spoon to constantly stir the custard as it heats to the proper temperature. As soon as the custard thickens and coats the spoons, strain through a fine-meshed sieve (there may be particles of cooked egg) and transfer immediately to a clean bowl set in another bowl filled with ice and stir until the custard is cool.

Industrial pasteurizing machines can be set to perform a high or low temperature process, depending on the type of mixture.

• Low temperature pasteurizing: The mixture is heated to 65 C (150 F) for 30 minutes then cooled quickly to 6 C

• High temperature pasteurizing: The mixture is heated to 82-85 C (185 F) for 3 minutes then cooled quickly to 6 C

4. Homogenizing

This process maintains the delicate emulsion of the coagulated proteins, fat and water that make up a custard. The mixture is slowly stirred to evenly distribute the solids throughout the mixture to give the final product a very smooth texture and rich flavor. Sometimes emulsifiers are added to help maintain the distribution of fat.

This process is best accomplished with a machine which agitates the mixture at a steady pace, hand stirring does not give the same results.

5. «Maturing»

Allowing an ice cream of sorbet mixture to chill completely for several hours (or up to 24 hours) before churning has several advantages:

• If the mixture contains stabilizers (usually gelatin based), they swell during this period and thicken the mixture making it light and increasing the volume.

• The flavor «matures» as the mixture sits in the refrigerator, the fat develops a smooth texture and a desirable acidity. The color and aromas develop as well.

This is not an obligatory step, but one that improves the quality of the finished product.

6. Churning

Churning is the step which gives the final texture to the product. The goal is to make an ice cream or sorbet which is smooth and thick and rich in flavor.

Whether done by hand or in a commercial churn, the mixture is chilled to freezing and stirred with two paddles which scrape the frozen particles form the sides of the bowl and distribute them into the liquid portion until the entire mass is frozen and thick with small ice crystals. Air is incorporated into the mixture making it light and creamy.

7. Quick freezing and storage

Water is the main element in all frozen confections. This water turns into tiny ice crystals during the churning process which help to separate the fat and protein and sugar particles, giving ice creams and sorbets a desirable texture.

If simply stored in a regular freezer, the product would dry out and loose some of its body after a short time.

Flash freezing to -20 C (-6 F) for at least one hour maintains the size of the ice crystals exactly as they were when the product was freshly churned. The crystals then stay in suspension and the product does not dry out.

Products can be stored at this temperature with little or no change in quality for some time. When they are placed in a regular freezing unit 0 C (32 F) to soften slightly, the texture and flavor is identical to the original product.

Identify Your Specific Needs

A. Restaurant

In a restaurant that serves 40-50 customers per day, it is obvious that a small churn is all that is needed to meet the demand.
It is worth the trouble however to make and churn a fresh batch of ice cream every day to serve on its own or as an accompaniment to another dessert. In some cases, depending on the rest of the menu, a pasteurizer or multi function machine, which can prepare savory sauces as well as ice cream mixtures, may be a good investment.

Otherwise the cooking of the mixtures should be done with great care on top of the stove. A small capacity churn equipped to work quickly is all that is needed.

Beware! Ice creams and sorbets which are not used at the end of service should not be melted and rechurned. The change in temperature could encourage bacterial growth.

For the preliminary preparation, much of the equipment needed to prepare ice cream and sorbets is used for making other preparations as well. For example; an accurate scale, a 5 quart mixer, dependable refrigerated units, refrigerated work surface. Space may be limited in a restaurant kitchen and while the frozen desserts can be prepared alongside the other pastries, there are certain rules to follow:

- Avoid contact with flour, separate the work stations or make flour-based doughs and custards at different times.

- Keep cartons that may be soiled on the bottom away from the preparation area.

- When service has started, set up the «mise en place» of sauces and garnishes in covered containers set in an ice bath.

For best results, a restaurant should follow the seasons, offering frozen desserts made with the best ingredients available at the time. Customers will appreciate the flavor and quality that come from the freshest ingredients.

B. Ice cream as a sideline in a bakery and/or pastry shop

In France, every bakery/pastry shop has regular clients who will appreciate being able to buy an ice cream cone or frozen dessert while buying their daily «baguette.»

Depending on the size of the shop, a multi-function machine is a good investment. Since it performs all the steps from cooking to pasteurizing to churning, it frees up the chef to manage the other parts of his business with no cross contamination.

Many of the mixtures used in French pastry can be made start to finish in this machine: pastry cream, flan, lemon cream, Bavarian cream, chocolate ganache, and many more.
This wonderful machine can also temper covering chocolate in large quantities for molded chocolates of all kinds for the holidays and for coating pastries.

The ice creams and sorbets can be combined with cream puffs, sponge cakes and meringues to make spectacular frozen desserts like profiteroles, «bûches» and «vacherins».

The owner must have a suitable freezer to store and display the frozen items.

The multi-function machine can also be used to make savory and hot sauces which are sometimes used for take out items.
Many French pastry chefs expand their businesses to include catering (many of the items have a pastry base like mini pizzas, «patty shells» filled with meat and sauce.) Many of the sauces, from tomato to mayonnaise can be made in the multi-function machine.

Some machines (like the Pastoglace from Autofrigor) can heat up to 120 C (250 F) to make caramel, jams, and fruit candies.

These machines also guard against contamination with a self contained mechanism which performs all the steps at the right temperature without as much handling or exposure to the air and other ingredients in the shop.

C. Frozen desserts as the main product in a tea room or «glacier»

A business that offers mainly frozen desserts will be equipped differently from those which make ice creams and sorbets as a sideline.

In order to offer the variety that the clientele expects of a specialty shop, the kitchen must be equipped and organized to prepare and store the products efficiently.
Even a small scale «glacier» requires a pasteurizer and several churns.

Attention must be paid to the formulas used to prepare each dessert so that the amount of sugar and stabilizer is just right to maintain a desirable texture.

It is essential to organize the preparation and storage so that each flavor of ice cream and sorbet is rotated and made fresh at even intervals.

If all the steps are followed according to the government guidelines, the taste and texture of the product will be perfect when served to the public, whether in a cone, as a fancy restaurant presentation or as a frozen dessert.

The «glacier» must also keep his kitchen as hygienic as possible at all times. In addition to keeping the machines cleaned, he must also make sure that the work surfaces, scoops, display cases, etc. are impeccable.

With a larger production than the restaurateur or pastry chef, the «glacier» is in a position to take advantage of seasonal fruits to make large quantities of desserts while the flavor and price of produce is at its best.

Choosing equipment for ice cream making
Equipment used in making ice cream and sorbet

1. Pasteurizer

Ice creams and sorbets have become very refined in taste and texture over the last few decades thanks in part to the development of new machines which are now used to prepare the mixtures efficiently and with consistent results. Each step in the process and small scale as well as larger producers must observe the rules laid out by the French government.

Pasteurizing each mixture is required by law to insure that is safe for the public to consume. The heating process which destroys the bacteria also has the benefit of transforming the proteins and sugars and dispersing them throughout the mixture resulting in a smooth, rich texture.

When the pasteurizing process for ice cream is done by hand over the stove, the milk (cream/butter) is brought to a boil in a heavy pot then flavorings are added which infuse into the hot liquid. The hot milk is blended with the egg yolks and sugar and eventually the stabilizer (if using) and other flavorings.

While the chef is constantly stirring the mixture, it heated to 80-85 C (185 F) and kept at that temperature for 3 minutes. The thickened custard is then strained through a fine-meshed sieve and chilled immediately over ice. It is essential to continue stirring the mixture as it cools as a «skin» forms on the top and holds the heat in, risking to over cook the custard.

The hot (strained) custard can be poured directly into the churn to cool if the bowl of the churn is made to withstand the high temperature.

A pasteurizing machine is designed to accomplish the entire process without intervention and without risk of human error. To achieve the best results (creamy texture), the ingredients (especially the fats and sugars) must be blended with precision.

Thanks to the pasteurizer, the mixture is agitated as it is heated and cooled, homogenizing and incorporating a little air into it as it performs its more important task of killing bacteria.

At the temperatures necessary for pasteurization, the fats are broken down into minute globules and distributed evenly through the liquid. It is sometimes difficult to heat the custard to the proper temperature by hand without getting it too hot and actually scrambling the eggs.

The pasteurizing process also helps to «fix» the stabilizer (optional), which helps to keep the fats and protein in suspension in the liquid portion (like a mayonnaise.) The lecithin in the egg yolk also stabilizes the cooked mixture.

Once the mixture has been heated, the pasteurizer is then programmed to chill the mixture very quickly. The maturing process can take place in the machine or the custard can be transferred to a bowl and refrigerated for several hours so that the flavor and texture have a chance to develop and «mature».
The fats develop a faint yet desirable acidic flavor during the maturing process and this acidity helps to set the color and flavor.

2. Churn

the freezing operation performed by the churn is the final stage in establishing the flavor and texture of the ice cream or sorbet. All the preparation leads to this moment when the balance of sugar and proper cooking results in a smooth creamy product.
It is important to choose a churn which is adapted to the size and type of business.
If the churn is too big and the mixture only fills it halfway, the texture of the finished product will be too heavy, even if the mixture was perfectly prepared. Not enough air will be incorporated into the mixture as it is churned and it will be hard and difficult to remove from the machine.
If the churn is too small (a more solvable problem), time is lost in filling and emptying the machine. In a business where the profits rely on the efficiency of the operation, too small a churn can cost the business a lot of money.
For the individual who loves to make frozen desserts it is advisable to purchase a churn with its own freezing mechanism rather than relying on the bowl set inside a frozen insert or surrounded by ice and salt. Note that using a salt and ice mixture is no longer acceptable in commercial establishments in France. There are some small machines which will fit in the freezer, these give satisfactory results.
The hand crank method may be fun and quaint but the results will never be as luscious as with a powered machine.

The paddles of the machine should turn at an even pace and lightly scrape the sides of the bowl. As the fine ice crystals form on the sides during churning, the paddle, with its two «arms» will remove the layer of crystals and disperse them into the liquid portion.

This action should not be too slow nor too fast.
* Too fast: The mixture might separate into ice crystals and bits of fat and become very granular with a strong taste of butter.
Too slow: The mixture might become very icy and granular.

Commercial machines give consistent results by maintaining a constant temperature and churning speed. The chef need only determine the length of time the mixture is to be churned based on the amount.

Choose a churn with a removable bowl which is easy to clean. The churn must be taken apart and thoroughly cleaned at the end of each work day to meet government regulation.

Multi-function machine

This new generation of machine can do the work of the pasteurizer and the churn, taking less space and time to operate.

If used properly, this machine can accomplish many tasks, leaving the chef to create more personalized products and expand his business.

A computer is at the heart of this new machine. It can be programmed to heat the mixture according to the pasteurizing guidelines then immediately cool it with no risk of contamination. The maturing process can take place right in the same bowl, all the while stirring it and homogenizing the ingredients. With no intervention whatsoever, the ice cream or sorbet is then churned to perfection.

This miracle machine can be programmed to cook and chill any mixture at all—sweet or salty, hot or cold.

3. Flash freezer

Rapid deep freezing has become an indispensable part of the frozen confection industry.

a. What is flash freezing?

Flash freezing drops the temperature of a food product to -40 C in a very short time, in some cases in just a few minutes.

b. What purpose does this serve and how is it different from freezing at 0 C (32 F?)

Products with a high water content benefit greatly from flash freezing. If allowed to freeze slowly, the ice crystals which form are very large.

The ice crystals over time, will separate from the proteins and fats. The water eventually evaporates, leaving the product very dry and tasteless. Fruits rich in pectin will lose aroma, flavor and color.

With flash freezing, the drop in temperature is so fast that large ice crystals do not have time to form. The ice crystals are very small and remained suspended evenly throughout the product, keeping it virtually unchanged even when softened enough to eat.

In large commercial production, flash freezing is now obligatory in France, which insures that the frozen products are bacteria free and high in flavor. being able to stock products with no change in texture and flavor also benefits the consumer. Larger quantities can be made at a time which lowers the price and a larger selection of flavors can be kept on hand.

The flash frozen items are then stored at -20 C (-45 F) until ready to be sold.

Freezers are now available in France which combine the flash freezing unit with a storage unit so the product can be easily moved from one part of the freezer to the other.

c. Why flash freezing/

The average ratio of liquid to solid in an ice cream or sorbet is about 65%.

When the ice cream or sorbet is removed from the churn only about half of this water is transformed into ice crystals. Flash freezing quickly freezes the remaining water so that large, grainy ice crystals do not form.

4. Equipment for pastries

To make a variety of frozen desserts, the «glacier» must make sponge cakes, cookies, meringues and more. To make these baked goods efficiently and well, basic equipment is needed.

The chef must decide on the level of quality he can afford and determine which to purchase based on the volume that each piece of equipment can produce.

The basic equipment includes:

A. Oven

The glacier» uses the oven to bake cakes, meringues and brown the top of «Baked Alaskas.» For a small operation it is advisable to choose a convection/conventional oven which can toast items to order and bake large items evenly. Place the oven away from work areas that must be kept cool.

B. Mixer

Indispensable for the blending of cake batter and beating meringues. match the size of the bowl to the size of the average amount of batter to be made (5-10 liters (about 5-10 quarts) is sufficient for most small businesses. Clients like to have a choice when it comes to ice creams and often it is best to make many small batches of different flavors than to make large amounts of only a few.

C. Whipped cream dispenser

a. Small dispenser: Hand held dispensers can be used but run out quickly and can be expensive.

b. Larger machines: These are practical for a shop that specializes in ice cream sundaes which requires a whipped cream decoration. Equipped with a sufficient refrigerated unit, it automatically whips the cream as it dispenses it.

D. Scale

Absolutely necessary for accurately weighing ingredients to achieve the correct balance of sweetness. Correctly measuring ingredients influences the quality and insures that the profit margin is consistent.

The scale should be checked for accuracy on a regular basis and cleaned thoroughly to eliminate any chance of contamination.

E. Stovetop

Choose the type that best suits your production and budget:

a. Gas: Sometimes the heat is not as strong as electric. Easy to use and to control.

b. Electric: More expensive in France. High, even heat, but hard to control.

c. Flat top: A very desirable alternative, easy to clean, high even heat. In France, this form of stovetop remains quite expensive.

Choosing equipment - Choosing a Pasteurizer

How does one use this machine?

The pasteurizer was developed to blend mixtures for ice cream and sorbets as well as syrups, sauces and creamy mixtures of all kinds.

Any liquid which can withstand the stirring action of the machine can be chilled in the pasteurizer. The standard machine is programmed to heat mixtures up to 120 C (250 F) and can maintain that temperature for up 2 hours. The machine can then rapidly drop the temperature of the bowl to 4 C (just above freezing) to quickly cool the mixture and maintain this temperature while the mixture «matures» and develops flavor. Some machines are equipped to then churn the mixture at -20 c (-45 F.)

Many establishments find this to be a practical alternative to processing the mixtures by hand.

What a pasteurizer cannot do.

Any preparation which requires a cooking temperature over 120 C (250 F) cannot be safely prepared in a pasteurizer. Also, many mixtures are too thick for the paddle of this machine to stir. Some multi-function machines are equipped to cook at a higher temperature and can manage stiffer mixtures.

Pasteurization at both the lower and higher temperatures required by French law are possible in this machine. Jam glazes and chocolate ganache do very well in this machine.

Slow cooking jams and fruit sauces can also be made in the pasteurizer.

Savory sauces such as béchamel and stocks can also be made.

Example of uses:

The pasteurizing machine is primarily used to make sauces, chill them quickly and hold them at a refrigerated temperature while the flavor develops.
• Low temperature pasteurizing at 65 C (148 F) for 30 minutes, then «maturing» at 4 C (40 F.)
• High temperature pasteurizing at 85 C (185 F) for 3 minutes.

Characteristics

The bowl of the pasteurizer is round which facilitates the agitation of the mixture for better homogenization. it is also easy to clean.

186

It is recommended to choose a machine that can be taken apart so that it can be completely cleaned.

All these machines require a reliable electrical source as it draws a lot of current. However, the automated cycles uses only the power needed to complete the task.

Water will condense and drip from the machine over a period of time. The recipient designed to catch the small amount of moisture should be emptied and cleaned daily.

Production

Machine capacity

The usefulness of a machine is a combination of the capacity, power and diversity of functions. The speed with which it performs certain steps is also an important consideration.

Example A (4-12 liters (about 5-14 qts))

The «MULTILAB 12 Glacier» can process 4-12 liters of finished product. The basic cycle is one hour and the «maturing» process can last as long as needed.

Example B (8-22 liters (about 10-26 qts))

The «PASTOMAT 20 Glacier» produces from 8-22 liters in just 80 minutes. In one day, it can produce 130 liters (about 150 qts.)

Example C (25-55 liters (about 30-65 qts))

If used in conjunction with a maturing machine of the same capacity, the PASTOMAT of this size can produce 400-450 liters (about 500 qts) per day.

Example D (50-110 liters (about 60-130 qts))

This PASTOMAT 100 machine is used along side maturing machines and churns of equal capacity to produce 600-700 liters (720-850 qts) per day. Four to five flavors can be made in a day.

Using a Pasteurizing Machine

Advice for installation

A pasteurizing machine should be placed in a cool, well ventilated spot where it can be cleaned easily.

Programming the production cycles

Pasteurizing machines in general are equipped with a micro-
computer which automatically executes the steps involved in
the pasteurizing process.
The MULTI LAB and PASTOMAT AUTOFROGOR machines
shown here can be programmed in advance to perform several
tasks in succession.
Once a mixture is pasteurized according to government regulations, the machine will maintain the temperature to complete the
«maturing» process as well.

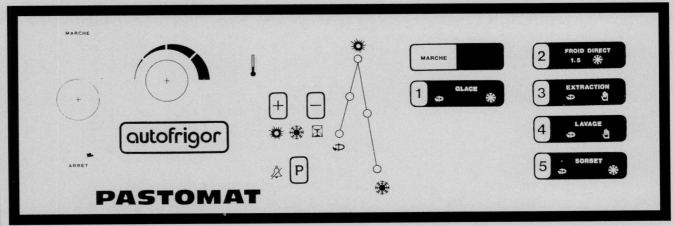

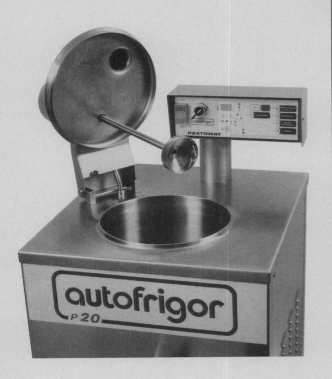

Control panel of a pasteurizer

Program for ice cream

Mixtures containing cream and eggs are programmed for a high
temperature pasteurization.

Cycle 1 begins the stirring motion and heats the mixture to 83
C (about 185 F) and maintains the temperature of the mixture
for 3 minutes.

Automatically, the mixture is quickly cooled to 4 C (45 F) and
can be held at that temperature to «mature» until the chef is
ready to churn.

Program for sorbet

Sorbet mixtures undergo a low temperature pasteurization which heats the mixtures to 65 C (about 165 F) and maintains that
temperature for 30 minutes. A higher temperature would destroy the aroma of the fruits. The mixture is then quickly cooled
to 4 C (45 F) and can be maintained at that temperature until
it is churned.

Chilling mixtures directly

Some producers may use the pasteurizing machine occasionally as a convenient cooling device for small quantities of custard
that is cooked on the stovetop then placed directly into the pasteurizer instead of chilling over an ice bath.

This machines can be used for some sorbets do not require a pasteurizing process but should be cooled quickly when the hot
syrup is added.

Equipment for making ice cream - Choosing a Churn

What can be done with this machine?

The main function of the churn is to freeze the mixture and turn it from a liquid to a solid. If the mixture is well made, the stirring action of the churn transforms the mixture into a smooth, creamy dessert.

Most churns are designed to receive a freshly cooked mixture (still hot) and cool it quickly before the actual freezing/churning process. If pasteurizing is done with care on the stovetop, the quick cooling action of the churn completes the pasteurizing cycle and replaces the need for a bowl of ice for chilling the mixture quickly. Therefore a churn can work in the place of a pasteurizer for the second half of the process and keep the mixture at a safe, chilled temperature.

What cannot be done with this machine?

The mixtures should not be chilled too rapidly. Thick mixtures especially should be gradually chilled. Quickly chilled, any mixture will be heavy and difficult to remove form the machine. If the mixture is gradually chilled then «matured» in the churn at 4 C (45 F) for several hours then slowly cooled to freezing, the product will be creamy and smooth. The taste will benefit as well from a slow chilling process.

Examples of uses

A variety of flavors can be churned in the course of one day if they are processed in order of color and flavor; from light to dark. The bowl can be emptied without the need to disassemble and clean.
The preparation can be timed so that as one mixture is finished in the churn the next is freshly cooked; this eliminates the step of storing the mixtures if the refrigeration in between steps.

Characteristics

The churns made by AUTOFRIGOR CLASSIC and the TRONIC are equipped to churn the mixtures at two speeds, the churn stirs more slowly at first then speeds up a little at the end to aid in removing the frozen mixture automatically to a container positioned outside the machine.
Smaller models usually have just one speed and the frozen mixture must be removed by hand.

The larger machines are approximately twice as powerful as the smaller ones, drawing on twice the power to operate them. Larger machines will take up slightly more room in the kitchen. Larger machines also require a water supply directly hooked up to the machine.

Production

Production volume

The AUTOFRIGOR churn can produce the following volumes (depending on the number of flavors.)

Example A (1-2 liters (1-2 qts)) (Small restaurants)

Up to 20 liters (about 25 qts) and 5-6 different flavors can be produced per day (a variety can be made by making a vanilla base and flavoring it with coffee, chocolate, etc.)

Example B (4-8 liters (about 5-10 qts)) (Large restaurants)

A large restaurant may need up to 300 liters (400 qts) per day, usually offering only a few flavors.

Example C (14-20 liters (about 15-25 qts) (Ice cream shop)

The volume depends on the extent of the variety and the amount of storage. More variety usually means lower production volume overall.
Up to 600-700 liters (about 700-825 qts) in as many 10-12 flavors can be churned each day with a machine of large capacity.

Vertical churns, such as this one, are equipped with a tall bowl like the traditional machines and can churn mixtures at a lower temperature which results in a creamier texture.

Using an Ice Cream Churn

Installation

Ice cream churns should be installed in a cool, well ventilated place, in accordance with all local health codes.

The location should be meet the standards for food preparation and be next to a water source so that the machine can be emptied and cleaned thoroughly and efficiently.

Safety and cleanliness are the important considerations when choosing a place to install an ice cream churn in a professional establishment.

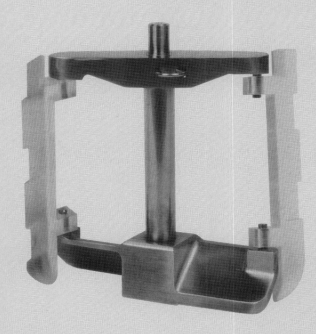

Functions of an ice cream churn

The mixture is poured into the bowl of the churn. It should fill the bowl about 1/2-2/3, depending on the mixture, to allow for the expansion that takes place during.

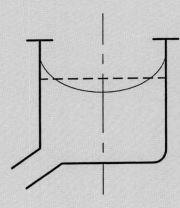 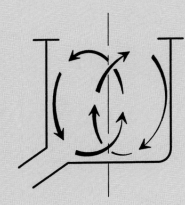 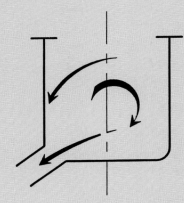

1. The mixture is gently stirred at the beginning of the churning process as the sides of the bowl begin to cool to down.

2. As the mixture begins to freeze on the sides of the bowl, the paddles scrape the sides and distribute the frozen mixture throughout the liquid portion.

3. When the mixture is perfectly churned, a valve is opened at the base of the churn and the action of the paddles automatically pushes the frozen mixture out of the machine.

Obtaining volume and creamy texture

Only a well made mixture will achieve volume and a creamy texture. Creamy mixtures, with or without eggs are more easily aerated and take on more volume than sorbets.

The controlled freezing and stirring process of a professional churn is another key to a light, creamy texture.

The volume and texture can be regulated to some extent depending on the type of frozen dessert that will be made from the frozen mixture; some layered desserts, for example, may slice better if the mixture is slightly more dense and ice cream can be more easily scooped if lighter in texture. By increasing the speed of the paddles for a few minutes at the end of the churning process, the volume can be slightly increased resulting in a lighter texture.

189

Choosing a Multi-Function Machine

What can be done with this machine?

The main advantage of this machine is that it can be used to prepare mixtures of all kinds. In addition to ice creams and sorbets, this machine will blend and cook to perfection pastry cream, ganache, flan (for the pastry chef), will temper covering chocolate, prepare caramel and fruit jellies (for the candy maker), prepare sauces such as bechamel and velouté (for the «cuisine» chef) and make aspic and sauces (for caterers.)

Even in a shop that sells only ice cream-based desserts, the multi-function machine replaces the pasteurizer and churn in one unit and can be used to some of the other preparations (cookies, cakes) that are used in making frozen desserts.

What cannot be done with this machine?

This machine can mix, cook and chill just about any liquid mixture.

To achieve maximum results, the chef should organize his work to make only sweet and savory preparations on alternate days so that the machine does is dismantled for cleaning only once daily.

Examples of uses

Chefs can offer a wider selection of desserts on the menu because the preparation time is reduced.

Several pastry fillings can be quickly prepared in the morning for the pastry chef to use throughout the day.

Next, the pastry chef can easily prepare chocolate and cookies to be served with the ice cream desserts.

In the afternoon, the chef can then proceed with the mixing and churning of ice creams and sorbets to be served by restaurant or tea salon.

Characteristics

These machines can be programmed to automatically cook, chill and, if needed, freeze any type of liquid mixture. No intervention is necessary, insuring a finished product that is the same quality each time, prepared in the most hygienic way.

The cooking cycle can heat a mixture to 120 C (250 F) and maintain this temperature for up to 2 hours.

The cycles can be determined with absolute accuracy so that the preparation is as goo as «homemade».

Once cooked, the mixture is cooled rapidly. Depending on the recipe, the temperature can be dropped to -3 (-27 F) C or -20 (-45 F.)

The size of the machine corresponds to the capacity. A machine which produces 4-30 liters (about 5-35 qts) an hour occupies about .5 X .65 meters (about 1.5 X 2 feet.)

Production

Examples

PASTOGLACE machines are available in four sizes.

• PASTOGLACE 8.20

Produces 2-4 liters (about 2-4.5 qts) per cycle, 8-20 liters (about 9.5-24 qts) per hour, depending on the recipe. Cycle is 10-30 minutes.

• PASTOGLACE 12.30

Produces 2-6 liters (about 2-7.2 qts) per cycle,12-30 liters (about 14-35 qts) per hour.
This is the most popular model among professionals..

• PASTOGLACE 24.60

Produces 4-12 liters (about 4.5-14 qts) per cycle, 24-60 liters (about 29-72 qts) per hour.

• PASTOGLACE 40.100

Produces 10-20 liters (about 12-24 qts) per cycle, 40-100 (about 48-120 qts) per hour.

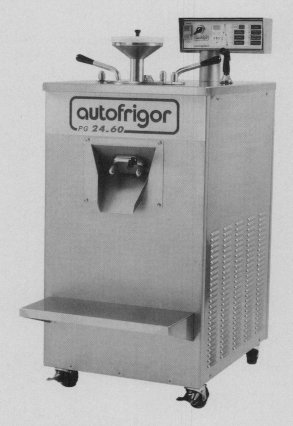

Using a Multi-Function Machine

Installation

Like all machines which make ice cream, this machine must be installed in a cool, well ventilated area which meets local health codes. The air-cooled models must have sufficient room around them and be placed where the heat of the machine won't warm the production kitchen. Water-cooled machine must be equipped with a recipient to catch condensation.

The «glace» (ice cream) function

The button on the control panel marked «glace» (ice cream) will cook and pasteurize the mixture followed by a freezing and churning cycle.

The mixture is stirred and heated to 83 C (about 185 F) for 3 minutes (temperature and time can be regulated), chilled, frozen and kept at the right temperature until the machine is emptied.

The «crème pâtissiere» (pastry cream) function

The button on the control panel marked «crème pâtissiere (pastry cream) adapts the machine to prepare thick mixtures. This function comprises a pasteurizing cycle followed by an automatic cooling cycle. During the refrigerated cycle, the mixture is stirred occasionally

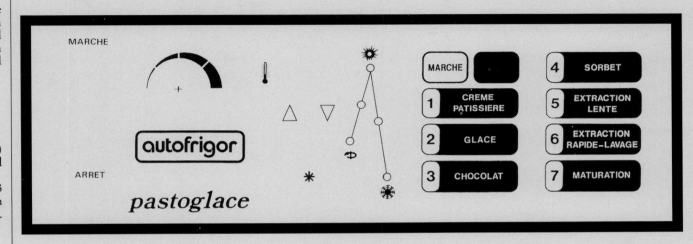

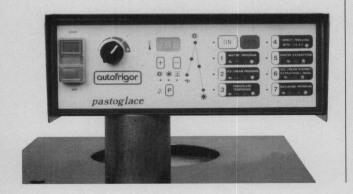

The «maturation» (maturing) function

The button on the control panel marked «maturation» (maturing) is a pasteurizing function which can be regulated to heat the mixture to a specific temperature, cooled automatically then held at the refrigerated temperature (usually several hours) so that the mixture can «mature», allowing the flavors and texture to develop. To freeze and churn the mixture, the «sorbet» function is activated».

The «chocolat» function"

The button on the control panel marked «chocolat» is programmed to automatically temper any type of covering chocolate (white, milk, dark) to prepare it for candy making. Chocolate in pieces or chopped is placed in the machine, After melting, the chocolate is heated to 45-50 C (130 F) for about 3 minutes then tempered according to the type of chocolate. The tempered chocolate pours out of the machine ready to mold or use as a coating..

The «sorbet» function

The button on the control panel marked «sorbet» is also cold «direct cold». This is a freezing function only, for those preparations that do not need to be cooked, pasteurized or «matured».

Any mixture ready for churning can be added to the machine and programmed for «sorbet».

Removal of the finished product

The machine can be programmed to expel the finished product slowly or more rapidly depending on texture of the product.

A cleaning function («lavage») follows the «extraction rapide». Cleaning and disinfecting products are added to the bowl and the machine then the «lavage» (cleaning) function is activated.

191

Hygiene in Ice Cream Making

Following proper rules of hygiene is one of the most important parts of all cooking operations, especially «glacerie». Keeping the kitchen and equipment in clean, working order and preparing the mixtures according to the standards becomes routine in a well run kitchen and the issue of «hygiene» does not keep the chef from working quickly and profitably. With fresh, unblemished ingredients and careful preparation, frozen desserts can be made with no health risks.

Organizing the work

Keep all ingredients that need to be refrigerated well chilled until ready to process, even if they are to be cooked and pasteurized.

Prepare just one mixture at a time to avoid cross contamination from spoons, bowls, etc.

When making specialty desserts, prepare the recipe in quantities that will fill the molds without leftover product.

Pay special attention to the measuring of stabilizers and emulsifiers (check the instructions on the specific product used.)

Choosing ingredients

Choose only the freshest ingredients for making ice cream. Check the dates on milk, cream, eggs, butter and maintain freshness of other ingredients such as stabilizers, and flavorings by purchasing in small enough quantities to insure a regular turnover.

Using more of an inferior product does not equal the right amount of a superior product.

Remember that the final quality in texture and flavor of the product relies on the perfect balance of ingredients.

Use the hygrometer to check the density of mixtures to make sure that the right balance has been achieved.

Locations and equipment

It is sometimes difficult to dedicate one room exclusively to the making of ice cream. The area used for preparing ice cream should always meet the strictest health code standards.

Walls and floors of the production area should be smooth and easily washed. The entire area should be cool and well ventilated.

The equipment should be rinsed after every preparation, completely cleaned and disinfected daily and thoroughly checked on a regular basis to keep it good working order.

After a thorough cleaning with a brush, rinse with clean water and leave to air dry.

Personal hygiene

A major source of contamination is the food handler. Everyone working in the kitchen must be trained to follow the necessary guidelines for proper hygiene.

Proper and clean attire should be worn at all times.

Hands should be washed following every preparation and each and every visit to the lavatory.

To be sure that your operation is in compliance with local regulations, contact your Board of Health.

About the Artist

The watercolors in this volume were created by artist Arlette Goubier, born in Lyon in 1941. As a yougster in her beloved Saône region near Lyon, she watched her father, an architect, at work and learned how to draw in perspective. Her watercolors illustrate this technical talent as well as her love of her native countryside. The beautiful cities of Lyon and Venice are her favorite subjects which she portrays in scenes that are cal and filled with light. Artist Goubier especially likes painting scenes with water and capturing the glistening lights on the surface. She is a member of the "Atelier Floréal à Dardilly" and often exhibits in the region. Arlette Goubier also spends a lot of her time teaching youngsters to enjoy the arts.

Translation

Translator Anne Sterling is a graduate and the former director of LaVarenne Ecole de Cuisine with over two decades of culinary experience. She is a food columnist, recipe consultant and teaches cooking to adults and children.

Photography Credits

The photographs in this book were taken by Pierre Michalet (except for Pages 84 to 87 and 122 to 125)

WILEY

ISBN 0-471-16066-3

John Wiley & Sons, Inc.
Professional, Reference and Trade Group
605 Third Avenue, New York, N.Y. 10158-0012
New York • Chichester • Brisbane • Toronto • Singapore

CICEM S.A.
36, rue St-Louis-en-l'Ile
75004 PARIS

ISBN 2-86871-004-8

Dépôt Légal 3ᵉ Tr. 97
Photogravure : FOTIMPRIM (Paris)
Photocomposition : BOA (Paris)
Impression et reliure : INTERLITHO (Italie)